FUNDAMENTAL
The Transforming Power of Having Fun

Copyright © 2016 Ryan Andrews

All rights reserved.

Published in the United States by DreamSurf Studio Publishing. Except as permitted under the United States Copyright Act of 1976, no part of this publication may be reproduced or distributed in any form or by any means, or stored in a database or retrieval system, without prior written permission by the publisher.

Library of Congress Cataloging-in-Publication Application 1-4103262531

Andrews, Ryan

Fundamental: The transforming power of having fun / Ryan Andrews – 1st ed.

ISBN 978-0-9983068-0-3

Printed in the United States of America

Design by DreamSurf Studio

FIRST EDITION

To my wife Nissa,
who never stops believing in me;
and our four amazing children.

CONTENTS

Introduction 5

01 My Story 8

02 Having Fun 18

03 Challenging Fun 34

04 Prioritizing Fun 50

05 Empowering Fun 72

06 Transforming Fun 90

07 Healing Fun 110

08 Your Story 128

09 Fun Extras 148

Notes 160

A NOTE TO MY READERS

I struggled for many years to give myself and my family everything we ever wanted only to find out that what we've always wanted doesn't cost a penny. We want to enjoy life.

I want to be happy and carefree, and my kids want their dad to be around for all their life accomplishments and the times when they don't quite make it. My wife wants me to be healthy and happy and spend quality time with her. What we are after is happiness and joy and a sense of adventure in everyday life.

What I found is that striving is like trying to swim by splashing around in the water struggling to keep your head above it. The thing is that in order to swim you must put your face in the water and breath in rhythm with your effort. When you do that, it's really fun to swim. When you don't, it's really stressful, fearful and tiresome.

Life is the same way, when we work furiously and push ourselves to the max all the time, it's striving to survive. Learning how to enjoy the process, and take advantage of the blessings around us, is like breathing in rhythm with your effort.

Here's the key: happiness doesn't come from success; instead, success comes from a place of happiness. It's when we enjoy our lives that we stop striving and start succeeding.

If you put those two things together, you get the basic direction of this book. First learn to enjoy your life, then mastering your life is simple.

The current fundamental understanding of how to become successful is to dedicate all that you have to something for as long as it takes, then you can enjoy life. This is backward, the people who are truly successful learned how to enjoy life through the process and never do something for too long that doesn't add to their overall enjoyment of life. It's our passion that keeps us going through the times that smiling is difficult. It's the love for our "WHY" that drives us to success.

In this book, I share stories of how I went from having the "perfect life" yet somehow I was still miserable to finding joy, peace, and prosperity in all areas of my life by simply learning how to have fun in the process.

My goal is to simplify the process of learning how to enjoy life. Even though the plan and the process is simple the road can often be difficult. This book is a kind of guide by way of my own life wins and life failures by which you can apply what worked for me and avoid what I did wrong.

I talk about my own addiction to food and how I broke free from it. I share about my struggles as a dad and how I over came them. I wrote about my failures as a husband and how the amazing power of having fun helped me fall in love with my wife more than ever before.

I believe that we all have a story to tell called life. Your story will be different than my story but the process is likely to be similar. Take the good stuff and apply it.

There is no magic bullet. Or in the words of Po from *Kung Fu Panda*, "There is no secret ingredient." Everything that you need to be successful at mastering your life is already inside of you. You are strong enough, brave enough, special enough and worthy to live the life that you've always wanted.

If there is one thing that I have found to be true it's this, people are resilient. We can take a major hit and somehow recover from it. Sure, there may be scars and we may never be the same again, but we will continue to fight and win.

When you finish this book I would love to hear from you. I would love to hear about the things I got right and how your life has been impacted. Send me an email or connect on social media.

www.ryan8.com

God bless!

Chapter 1
MY STORY

fun·da·men·tal – a basic principle, rule, law, or the like, that serves as the groundwork of a system; essential part

I was living in Hawaii with my smokin' hot, amazingly powerful wife and our three kids, I worked for myself, we owned rental property, I was the worship pastor at my church…and I was miserable. I had everything I had ever dreamed of, yet all I wanted to do was crawl into a hole and hide.

It was 2013 and I was under tremendous financial pressure. This wasn't new to me; I had survived this before. In fact, the story of how we got to Hawaii is quite amazing but all at once I was overwhelmed with fear and doubt and I was not enjoying my life.

There wasn't one thing to put my finger on, but I could feel myself slipping away slowly. The pain of being less connected and less in tune with my own passions was becoming real. It was like I was a machine. Work, work, work, go home, kiss the wife, yell at the kids, go to bed. Where had the happy guy gone? Where was that love for life that I remember? Who am I? How did I get here? Do I matter? Does anyone care?

One day while working I called my wife with this realization: "Honey, I don't know why, but I'm not happy." Silence on the other side of the phone told me that she was waiting for the bomb to drop, so I clarified. "You are amazing, and the kids are awesome but for some reason I'm just not happy. Will you pray for me?" She agreed and we talked briefly a bit longer and then I went right back to finishing my work for the day.

In our marriage up to that point, I was always positive and ready to see the bright side. I also didn't share with my wife much about any struggles I was having. So, for her to get this call meant that something was seriously wrong. Despite the heaviness of the conversation, I had no idea why I wasn't happy; I just knew that I was dying a little inside every day.

A LITTLE BACKSTORY

As long as I can remember I've been the "fun guy." My mom used to call me Mr. Happy, and I was quoted in a magazine at 12-years old saying, "Why would anyone think negative when they can choose to think positive?"

If I go far enough back, I had a rough go. My parents were divorced from the time I was 2 years old. I only got to see my Dad every other weekend and my Mom worked as hard as she could just to pay the bills and keep food on the table. So, my time with her wasn't ideal either.

I could have easily been the *sad* guy. As a child I remember one occasion screaming at my Mom in the hall, and a couple of times saying horrible things to my Dad. I mean, take a big scoop of emotional pain. Add in an undeveloped brain and emotional core. Stir it all together with a dash of instability and pour a bunch of stress on top. That is a recipe to every cliché in the book for a rage-o-holic high school dropout. BUT, that wasn't my story.

Instead, I listened

My Mom started to get into motivational speakers and we had

every Zig Ziglar tape you could find. She would play them in the car over and over again. Dale Carnegie, Brian Tracy, Jim Rohn, Napoleon Hill, Stephen Covey (he came later), and an unknown to most Robert J. Sturner were my mentors.

Every seminar, tape and quote that my Mom shared with me I listened. I thought about it, I processed it, and at 10-years old I believed them. It made sense. I didn't understand that it was a struggle for adults to think the way these mentors told us to think. If they said happiness was a choice, then I decided to be happy. If they told me, how I wanted my life to go was completely up to me, then I started to make my plans. I was a student of positivity.

I always had friends, and it was always easy for me to make new ones. In high school, I hung out with the Christian kids, and I was a jock; I loved science and math so I spent a lot of time with the nerds, and one of my best friends was an atheist raised by a witch (seriously). I made it a point to be friendly to the goth kids, and I always stuck up for the mentally challenged kids. Just about everyone liked me OR they hated me because everyone else liked me. It's probably no surprise when at the age of 11 I read Dale Carnegie's, *How to Win Friends and Influence People*.

I learned the art of perspective, and what it means to frame life in away that's worth living. I discovered the power of reframing and whenever I did get in trouble for doing stupid kid things, I could always talk my way out of it. When I was 17 I saw a book, *How to Be Rich* by J Paul Getty and thought, "That sounds like a good thing to know." So, I read it and applied it to my life.

As you can see I had all the training necessary to have the right frame of mind and be in a good place for my whole life. So, why was I depressed? This was shocking even to me! Other people deal with depression, but not me! Not "Mr. Happy." Yet there I was, with a perfect life, under a cloud of stress, shame and self doubt.

BACK TO MY STORY

Every day I slipped further and further down. My work suffered, but I was still consistent. I was a total ass to my wife and kids through it all (I'm sorry, guys). Then, one day I heard God say, "Ryan, joy comes from the inside not the outside."

And just like that, all of my training I had begun as a child came flooding back to me. I mean, I had instilled philosophies from the time I was a kid to believe that life is what you make it. Of course! How did I forget?! I'm not exaggerating that within an hour I was singing to the radio with the windows down. Someone from church caught me dancing in the car to the music. The depression had lifted.

That's when I started developing my life philosophy.

You get ONE shot at life. That's it!

You're only 23 ONCE

You're only 30, 35, 46, 50, 62 ONCE!!!!

You only have today, there's no yesterday, and there's no tomorrow. You only own RIGHT NOW, so what are you going to do with it!?

Your disposition is yours: It's your choice, perspective, mindset, identity, and training.

I have discovered the secret to being happy with little and with much and it's ALL the same thing. Choose to be happy.

> Life is a gift. If you don't enjoy it while you have the chance, you may go to your grave having never really lived.

I will explain a bit more on this later, but if there's one thing you get from this whole book, know that it's never too late to start being happy and having happy people around you. Your life is your own and your past does not predict your future unless you let it. If you don't like where your life is going then make a change. It's NEVER too late to start.

SO WHY WAS I MISERABLE

It's surprisingly simple. I had worked so hard for so long and under so much financial stress that I had removed my body's ability to enjoy life. I know that sounds crazy but it's scientifically true. There are many studies which show that prolonged exposure to stress reduces the dopamine receptors in your brain. What that means is your body cannot receive the benefits of having fun.

Dopamine is a motivator for taking action. Fulfilling goals, needs and desires produce pleasure for achieving them in the form of dopamine. Low levels of dopamine or a smaller number of dopamine receptors leads to procrastination, low self esteem and being unhappy. If you are procrastinating, experiencing self-doubt or low self-esteem and a lack of enthusiasm then you are probably low on dopamine.

Studies on rats showed that those with low levels of dopamine always opted for the easy way out and suffered because of it by receiving less food. Even though they knew they were going to get less food, they would still continue to choose the easier path that led to starvation. Those with higher levels of dopamine exerted the effort needed to receive twice the amount of food and consequently were healthy and happy.

In working so hard and going through years of financial stress, I inadvertently made it impossible for me to enjoy the life I created. This is why even though I had everything I had ever dreamed of, all I wanted to do was crawl into a hole and hide. I created this reality for myself.

There I was, the guy that was so good at having fun, and enjoying life. My whole dream was to have a happy family and live somewhere amazing and do amazing things. I wanted to inspire people to greatness and show my kids what a life on fire looked like. Instead, I had created a life that was probably better without me in it, or at least that's what I thought.

Because I couldn't have fun, it didn't matter how awesome my wife was to me: it didn't change how I was feeling. She was so patient and understanding yet I didn't realize that I was destroying her a little every time I talked to her from my place of stress and pain. I couldn't see that my disposition and my words were breaking my kids down. To me, their actions were a direct attack on me. Not the truth that they too had needs, and they were seeking what I could easily fulfill for them.

A couple of years later, I realized what I was actually doing. Any need or issue that my wife or kids had felt like an attack; it was added pressure that I just couldn't cope with. My default reaction was yelling at the kids or making my wife feel stupid for even bringing things up to me. The damage was hardening their hearts and chipping away at them at the same time. My attitude was leading towards a destructive path where the kids wouldn't want me to be around them and potentially an ugly divorce. I don't want to say it's never too late to turn things around, but it's never too late to be the man or woman that you should be.

My wife married me because she loved me, and kids are more forgiving than can be expected, so to make a real change it took admitting I was out of control and to get help. I started talking with my wife about ALL of my struggles and challenges. I let her into the scary places of my heart and got really vulnerable. It was uncomfortable at first, but then I discovered what I should have always done from day one: let her be one with me. Once I started doing this, the kids were a lot easier, they each received a strong and sincere apology individually. With new actions and tools for coping we were back on track.

Amazingly enough, it was a simple mindset change that allowed me to start healing my biochemistry. There are actually a bunch of really cool chemicals that the body produces which are all designed for you to enjoy your life. We already talked a bit about dopamine but here are some others:

Serotonin is considered by some researchers as the "mood chemical." If you're feeling depressed or lonely, it's because this chemical is either in low supply or your body is having trouble receiving it. It comes from feeling significant or important.

This chemical release comes from positive experiences, and feelings of value. Consciously being grateful for things, Vitamin D, and having fun are all ways to boost serotonin levels. Telling stories of past experiences helps release serotonin but reliving the past in a bad way actually hinders your body's reception of serotonin.

Oxytocin creates intimacy, trust, and helps build relationships. It's released during orgasms, childbirth and breastfeeding. It has been proven to help men with fidelity. One study showed that men who were given a boost of oxytocin and were in a monogamous relationship interacted with single women at a more appropriate distance than men without the boost. In general it helps create improved social interactions. Receiving a gift raises oxytocin levels and it's fun to get and give a gift!

Endorphins are released in response to pain and stress and help to alleviate anxiety and depression. Laughter and exercise are the simplest ways to get those endorphins flowing. Even the anticipation of something funny can release them.

Pleasurable foods and smells all trigger a release of endorphins. Yep, dark chocolate and even spicy foods are two of the biggies. Smelling lavender and vanilla or smells that recall good memories help release them as well. Being full of endorphins boost the immune system, lower stress, and help you focus.

Once my body started to catch up with my newfound mindset, it was simple to start thinking clearly and begin the process of setting myself up for success. Be patient. It takes some time for the chemicals to start balancing back out, especially after years of being depleted.

Eating healthy helps a lot with this. Studies have shown that mega dosing on Niacin even as high as 150,000mg per day can help snap people out of depression. Obviously that is an extreme case, but taking 1000mg - 3000mg per day is probably enough for the average person. There are lots of foods that help with your body chemistry but you can't go wrong with some fresh fruit. One of my go-to's is a juicer and a lot of carrots.

HOW HARD I TRY

No matter how hard I tried, there was no way that just having the proper mindset was going to get me the life of bliss that I wanted. I firmly believe that once you make a mess, then you have to clean it up. Or in other words, once you make a discovery, then you have to finish digging it up. There was still a lot of work to be done if I wanted to keep my life free flowing.

I started making it a point to improve my attitude and relationship with my wife. I was more intentional about not being annoyed by the kids. I made it a priority to have fun being a dad. And most importantly, I was willing to change.

FREE DOWNLOAD

Ask yourself this, **"If I'm not enjoying my life, then why not?"** It can be helpful to write this down. Make a list of some of the things that feel out of your control and are also taking you a direction that you don't want to go. Be careful with these though, finish the book before making judgments on them. It's often not the things on this list that are the problem.

Download A FREE Worksheet: www.ryan8.com/fundamental

Chapter 2
HAVING FUN

fun - n. enjoyment, amusement, or lighthearted pleasure

I was the janitor at my church for a little while. One of my main tasks was to keep the restrooms clean. It was always gross, but I remember enjoying the job. I didn't really mind doing it, in fact I made it part of my morning prayer routine. It was the only place that no one would bother me, and it was very peaceful. So my mornings after a church gathering were spent in prayer and meditation. I also happened to be cleaning restrooms in the process.

Cleaning the toilet isn't fun. Cleaning a public restroom is even less fun, and cleaning a public restroom in a venue that gets thousands of people through it every weekend is probably one of the least fun things to do. The key here was simply that I had a priority of enjoying my time, and the fact that my job was gross and very unfun was irrelevant.

You could have a job that you hate or a marriage that is failing and simply shift your perspective, mix in a little daily fun, and transform those same things into a job that you enjoy and a fulfilling marriage. It's really that simple. The challenge comes from spending years doing it one way, and then starting to do it differently. It will take some effort and will be difficult at first but if you truly want a shift, then it's worth the awkward phases of challenging your perspective.

Fundamental to joy, happiness, and a life that you love is to have fun in everything that you are doing. There are a few principles that are appropriate to have as a core value for everything. One of those is to have fun. I would like to be clear: not everything you do will be fun. Some things require focus and training, or even pain and suffering. If the goal though is to enjoy your life, then you must prioritize having fun in everything that you do.

> "I have noticed that a man is usually about as happy as he has made up his mind to be."
>
> –Abraham Lincoln

THE FORMULA IS BACKWARDS

The formula I was taught by society is: WORK, WORK, WORK = Retire = maybe fun if I have enough energy or am healthy enough at that point. Having fun is childish, right? And it has no place in business. This thinking is completely backwards.

My oldest son Ezekiel plays traveling soccer and it forces us to take a trip out of town at least once a month. These trips are time consuming and costly and could very easily be considered a burden. For us, they aren't a burden and we enjoy our forced mini vacations. How it started was with a trip to Disneyland that went amazingly well.

My wife's dream was to take a family vacation to Disneyland, but my dream was to never take a family vacation to Disneyland. I had spent a lot of time there growing up and I just knew that if I took my family to the magic kingdom it would end up as a whining gripe fest. Somehow she talked me into taking everyone for Christmas one year.

I had made it clear that if I did this that everyone would give me extra grace for my poor demeanor and that I REALLY don't want to go. There were other trips, even small ones where I would go out of my way to do something amazing for the kids and they would complain and argue and fight the whole time. The last thing that I wanted was to take an expensive trip 600 miles away during an already stressful holiday time. The smiles and joy in the eyes of my children and really more my wife, won me over. I was right at the beginning stages of learning how to have fun. For some reason, I had it in my mind that this trip was going to end poorly for me.

The trip was an amazing success! I was calm and cool and collected. The kids were troopers and spent all day back to back to back walking around the park and going on all the rides. To save on expenses we brought our lunch in the car so we had to return to the parking lot at least once and sometimes twice a day to eat, refuel and return for more fun. I really did it! I was able to mitigate the meltdowns, and keep everyone enjoying the entire trip.

Writing this brings tears to my eyes because it would have never happened before. I had found the secret to enjoying life and it was starting to leak out onto my family. On the way back each kid individually made time to pull me aside and tell me that this was the best trip of their entire lives. It was way too expensive, and took much longer than I could afford to take off working but the payoff was priceless.

Previously we could take a trip to get frozen yogurt and it would end in disaster. Partially because I couldn't just let the kids be kids. And partially because kids know how to push your buttons. When I am trying to have fun as a part of every outing it just makes everyone's time that much better.

Even though fun is a key element to enjoying life, there are times when it's difficult to make it a priority. Sometimes we feel like it's immature, unacceptable or worse that it's frowned upon. There is a time and a place to be serious like a doctor delivering some tough news or a lawyer defending someone who is innocent. There are however, an equal amount of opportunities to have fun and enjoy life even in those professions.

Did you know that studies have shown that doctors are 19%

more likely to have an accurate diagnosis when they have a positive attitude? I don't know about you, but if I'm trying to get a diagnosis I would definitely want a doctor who knows how to have fun and enjoy life. If for no other reason than just to get my diagnosis correct.

The most effective teachers are those that know how to make learning fun. My kids and their friends tell me that they learn better when they are having fun, and it was the same for me in school. Although teaching is an important job, knowing when to have fun and when to be serious seems to be the most effective way to get through to kids.

There is a TedTalk by Tyler DeWitt where he is speaking about teaching science and how he discovered that the textbooks were impossible for the kids to learn from. He has made the lessons fun and breaks the text down into understandable versions. The result is that his students do better compared to others and go on to do more with science than others as well.

Having fun has the power to transform your life in a way that will create tools to be successful at everything you do. The same principles that help you learn better while having fun will be the same things that propel you to success.

One of the fun things I like to do when I go to the store is find something interesting or thoughtful to bring home to my wife. It could be some crazy new produce to try like Dragon Fruit or it could be a bar of expensive dark chocolate. I don't do it every time, yet almost always I'm naturally thinking about something that will enhance my life or the people around me by doing something unexpected.

The last time I was shopping at Trader Joe's, for instance, I bought my daughter a mini-rose bush. It cost me $3.49 but the look on her face was priceless. It's not about the price tag or even the stuff itself; it's about the purpose behind it all. I mean, does a 7 year-old girl need a mini rose bush?! Not really, but the point is she would have been just as happy playing and not getting the gift. It was the action of me giving her the gift, however, showing her that I was thinking of her, which created a cool bond between us and a fun story for her to tell her friends about her new roses.

The total cost monthly for me to do something like this for the most important people in my life is about $20. I would say that's worth every penny. It enhances my relationship with my family and it brings me pleasure to do something fun. And ultimately, isn't that the point of life? We are meant to enjoy it while we have the opportunity.

This brings me to one of my keys for having fun...

SYNCOPATION

I've been a musician for over 20 years now and can play over 10 instruments, so I find it fascinating to make discoveries that are relevant to everyday life in music. One of my discoveries came in the form of syncopation.

Syncopation is a musical term that refers to the beat of a song doing something unexpected. For example if you hear, da dum, da dum, da dum, your brain assumes the next phrase will be da dum. What makes music exciting is when it does something like da dum, da dum, da dum, da dum, dum, dum, dum. Of course it is not syncopation for the song to go out of beat. It must still be in rhythm with the song, but it just does something unexpected. Something as simple as a pause in the music can also be syncopation.

We do like to have some semblance of order in our music and our life called rhythm, but it's those unexpected moments that activate our brain. Otherwise, our brains are easily bored with the same thing over and over again like a work routine that never changes.

So what does that have to do with my life and my enjoyment of life?

Life is similar to music. There's a story being told, and the things we do and say are like the music. If we live a life that's out of control, it's like music that has no beat. It's chaos. Some people live from a place of pain and like a sad song we can empathize with them but we don't want to be around them too often. The same is true for happy people and their lives, they are fun to be around like a happy song on the radio that you just want to play over and over.

Life isn't just a series of events, it's a series of events in rhythm with our passions.

Example 1: If you found out that you won the lottery, you would likely be thrilled. Why? Partially because you would probably quit working the next day (or minute). But the real reason is because it was unexpected, and in this case very unexpected. You were going about your life planning, saving, and working hard to get to the next moment, then bingo! All your money problems were solved in one fell swoop.

Example 2: Let's say you're driving through your favorite coffee store and you get to the front after ordering and they hand you your drink. You go to pay them and they say, oh, no charge the person in front of you paid your bill for you because they wanted you to have a nice day. Yay!!! The same feeling of elation and enjoyment would flood over you. The same body chemicals that were released for the lottery would be released for the free coffee.

Is there a difference between winning the lottery and getting a free cup of coffee? Yes, in terms of longevity but not really in terms of body chemistry. We can all agree it would be nice to have a big windfall like the lottery. However, if you fast forward your life past the initial expenditures and you still have 30 million buckaroos in your bank. You could end up watching TV for a few days in a row and get bored. How could you possibly be bored with your life if you were instantly a millionaire? It's simple: the lack of syncopation. Your brain has no choice but to slip into boredom by the monotonous repetition.

NATURE

Another example of syncopation can be found in nature. The most beautiful wood in the world is usually categorized as one that has a complex grain and doesn't follow any specific pattern. Whether it's Figured Maple, Zebrawood, or even simple White Pine with a unique pattern, the subtle differences are what make it beautiful. The wood grain is interesting and beautiful because it's not the same exact pattern over and over again. Rather, it's when the grain has a unique or unexpected quality to it that we find it amazing to look at.

Water, fire, clouds, fields, mountains, ocean, lakes, forests, or even deserts are all intriguing to us because of their syncopation. If we happened upon a lake while hiking that is a perfect circle, it would actually be interesting because most lakes are not a perfect circle. If all lakes were a perfect circle, then seeing a square lake would blow our minds.

In humans, the #1 factor for being attractive is unique harmony between the two halves of the face. If you drew a line down the middle of someone's face from their hairline down to their chin would both halves match? The more identical they are, the more the person is considered attractive.

What isn't a factor is the dimensions of the features that the person has. A big nose, or a small nose, wide eyes or narrow eyes, strong chin or no chin isn't as important. When looking at super models for example, you will rarely see someone who looks like Barbie. Most models have a "unique" look, something that makes them stand out from the crowd. It's the unique qualities that make their pictures interesting to look at.

When I look at pictures of my wife from when we were first married, I find myself thinking how much more beautiful she is today. I have pondered how it is that I can look at the same person everyday and find her more attractive, and it's because as we age our looks change ever so slightly. Over time it makes for a syncopated experience that I continually find attractive. It doesn't mean she was less attractive before or that she is more attractive now, only that I find her more attractive everyday.

RHYTHM

The power of a strong routine is evident if you have children. Also, most successful people have a solid routine. I've found in my own life that if I have too much craziness that it's hard to concentrate. I realize that this seems counter intuitive to my syncopation argument, which I will straighten that out right now.

The key to syncopation is that it's unexpected.

In order to have something be unexpected there has to be repetition to lull your brain into thinking the next thing it sees will be more of the same. This is very true in music: we call it rhythm. Without rhythm, there can be no syncopation, and it would be very difficult to listen to. Think about a toddler mashing the keys on a piano; no rhythm but plenty of syncopation, and not enjoyable to anyone but the tiny composer.

Without a routine or consistent rhythm, life is simply chaos. This is where children make this the most evident. If you don't have kids you'll have to just believe me on this one: I have 4 and they are all PERFECT examples of this. If you do have kids then you've probably been nodding your head while you're reading this. Kids NEED routine and boundaries. When they don't have a solid routine they get crabby and fight with each other and do strange things like fill outlet plug holes up with play-dough (true story). Yet once you start to settle into a routine with them then they can act right.

For children almost everything they do is new. They are constantly learning and changing and growing, etc. They simply can't handle one more area of their life being out of rhythm. So when they have too much craziness they act out in the same way. Kids are really just exaggerated versions of adults, we have the same issues with chaos.

My wife can hardly function if the house is a mess, and if the kitchen is in need of a good cleaning, then it's difficult for her to be creative. I have found that I'm more productive when my desk is in order and I really am happier when the world around me is functioning in rhythm. Once everything is flowing well, then the unexpected things that present themselves are a joy to embrace.

7 STRANGE THINGS I DO TO MAKE LIFE FUN

When I first learned about syncopation, I didn't actually have a term for it. I was in a business meeting and the man speaking was talking about keeping life interesting. He suggested a few quirky things to do to change up your routine as a way of breaking up the monotony.

I decided to give it a go, and I started to really enjoy doing silly things to keep my routine playful. Here are a few things that I do regularly that are a great way to learn how to embrace the unexpected. You can come up with your own, or copy mine but either way I recommend adding some fun things like these into your normal daily routine.

1. Shave differently. Almost every time I shave, I start at a different place on my face. Sometimes I start at my lip, sometimes at my sideburn, other times below my chin. This is something I have done for over 15 years. It's simple and silly and lovely.

2. Take alternate routes to work. Drive a slightly different way to work every day. This one is awesome! I have a couple of stop signs and lights that I decide which way to go based on which light will be green first, or sometimes depending on my mood. It's a simple way to enjoy something unexpected that life throws at us.

3. Non-occasion gifts. Gifts are an amazing way to throw off someone else's routine. Simply buying a cup of coffee for the person in front of you at the local coffee shop. That's safe because you heard their order and know how much they are gonna cost you. If you really want to throw things off, pay for the person behind you. Shockem'!

I actually really like getting simple gifts for my wife when there is no occasion. Could be chocolate bar for $1 or a bouquet of flowers. Or my recent one (I have to admit, I'm pretty proud of this one), I sent her to Hawaii for 2 weeks to say, "Thanks for putting so much into our family and the kids, now go take a break. The kids are in school and have sports so it wouldn't have worked for all of us to go this time. Enjoy your Self!"

Again, the amount and the reason are relatively unimportant. It's all about the surprise!

4. Positive messages. Every day, message someone something encouraging. I do this with text message, or on Facebook or even email. If someone pops into your mind, send them a quick note. Even something simple like "You're Awesome!" is sufficient. My wife and I do this to each other a lot randomly. There's nothing better than getting a text from my wife that says "I Love You!!!"

5. Get Multi-Cultural. Speak a different language when ordering out somewhere. I'm from Hawaii so it's common for me to say "mahalo" (thank you). But it really throws people off, in a good way, because they are expecting English from this big white guy in front of them.

6. Try out different names. Change your name when placing an order for them to call out. I like doing this when making a dinner reservation. I will usually try to come up with something unique or a bit goofy. The looks on their faces when I say my name is "Cornelius" or "Maxamillion" probably boosts me up more than them! In fact, even when I'm writing it right now it makes me laugh because our long-term memory helps us relive those moments again and again. Sometimes I'll do something a little more low key and say my name is Barry Allen (The Flash) in an attempt to find a fellow comic book fan that would catch my DC Comics tribute. So far, no one has ever asked me if that was my real name, so I'll have to keep looking!

7. Dress differently. Getting dressed is a good place to try something crazy. I like to get dressed differently as well. If normally I put my pants on first, I will put my shirt on first. And then the next day I do the exact opposite. Or, if I normally wear black socks, I might try a blue or red pair. If you want to be sneaky then you could wear something wild underneath. I've found it's better if others can see it to spread the fun, but do what you can.

FUN ALL THE TIME

The question has been asked of me, how much "fun" are you allowed to have at your job? This is usually followed up with, "If you're fun all the time how do your children learn discipline?" Being married takes work, right? If we just pretend nothing is wrong and have fun how does that help? And you know what else, eating kale salads everyday for lunch isn't fun either so what are we talking about here?

First, I would like to say that the purpose is to make fun a priority. Don't make it a chore. I'm not talking about making life a giant party because honestly, that sounds absolutely exhausting. It's very easy to forget to have fun in the process of doing something difficult, required, mundane, or repetitive. It's in those moments that we grow the most, but remembering to have fun afterwards helps us recognize the purpose behind hard work.

If I had one life mission it would be to help the entire world see that life is a gift, and that it's a gift worth enjoying. The problem I see is that whereas most people and companies *believe* it's important for us to enjoy what we do for a living, the truth is their actions say that we need to stay professional and fun isn't acceptable. I used to wear all the right clothes to meetings. I made sure I was nice to my neighbors, and always have on the right face at the right times…..BOR-ING!

I started to wear bright colors, and fun belts or socks. I make sure that I'm dressed appropriate for the occasion but I also want to share my own personality with those around. Sometimes it's a crisp white shirt and other times it's a crazy multicolored party in print.

When we are bored there is a whole host of problems that occur inside the body both physiologically and emotionally. We turn into more of a zombie than a participant. If we try to live the life that is expected of us, will we ever really get it right anyway?

The truth is that expectations and being proper are good for keeping people in line but horrible for making people get engaged with their lives. If I'm doing all the right things at all the right times, life becomes predictable and more than likely I will not be thrilled with any hope for what's next to come. If I already know that it's going to be the same thing I did the time before my level of excitement will diminish and the quality of what I'm doing will diminish as well. There's no freedom to explore! I just want to be free to be me.

It's time to engage. You only get one shot at life, and fortunately it's *never* too late to start learning how to enjoy it.

TRUE TO ME

When I was going through my transformation process a few years ago, there were many times that I would speak with people that I thought would help me. One of the things that I said a lot was, "I just want to be me." I always felt like I wasn't free to be me. I found out later that wanting to be ourselves is a common sentiment. A lot of people feel like they aren't being true to themselves. In fact there is a field of study around something called *Impostor Syndrome*.

They have found that around 70% of people suffer from *Impostor Syndrome* on one level or another. To over simplify it, it's when people don't feel like they are being true to themselves. Typically it comes when someone has a measure of success and are afraid people will find out that they are not as good as everyone thinks they are. I don't want to get too heavy here, personally I believe that a lot of "issues" and "syndromes" are just a case of too much stress for too long, but for me I definitely felt like I was not allowed to be myself.

I've dealt with this on many levels with several different people and it's always the same things. I feel trapped, I feel lost, I feel invisible, I feel like I don't matter, I feel like no one listens to me, etc. The common theme here is "I feel."

Feelings are liars, they tell us what we want to hear. They reflect our biochemistry and what our subconscious is telling us. Our feelings are valuable and valid, but they are not the best leader to follow. I do not want to discount your feelings because they are good indicators of something going on but be careful if using your emotions as a guide to your life decisions, they often do not reflect truth.

Imagine it's 3 a.m. and you fell asleep about 11:45. You hear crying in the other room, a hacking cough and then… your 3 year old just threw up all over themselves and their bed and all their stuffed animals.

How do you feel?

This has happened on more than one occasion and I can tell you right now that I didn't really feel like getting up and dealing with it. My emotions swirled with frustration, annoyance and being grossed out. I was tossed all over the place by my emotions and what I was about to deal with.

Of course, I ignored my feelings and got up to deal with it. I cleaned the kid, got them in some new jammies and put them in our bed hoping they wouldn't have a second episode. I pulled all the sheets off the bed and took the soiled animals and pillows to the washer and started the wash. My feelings were a mixture of things from hoping it was a dream and everything was normal to plain ol' anger for being woken up in the middle of the night this way. But feelings are only reflections of what's going on inside. They aren't actions, nor are they indicators of who I am. If I followed my feelings, I could have been a horrible parent and made a bad decision about what to do.

Would you follow your feelings? The answer is hopefully, no. It's because feelings aren't always the best leaders. Just because we feel like doing or not doing something is irrelevant when the time comes to something important. In this example it is important that we take care of the child and make sure they will get quickly on the road to health.

When making the decision to have fun, you are giving your feelings something to focus on while you complete difficult or boring tasks. You help your feelings get in line with where you are going instead of being pulled around by them wherever they want to go.

I am in charge of who I represent myself to be and how the world interacts with me. If people treat me poorly, it's because I have trained them to act that way. In general people don't push me around:

I don't allow it. I'm not mean or tough about it, and I definitely don't bully or belittle them in the process, but I just don't allow it.

What I do allow is for people to have FUN around me. I set up my life and the interactions people have with me to be something fun and enjoyable. I'm always smiling. Life is more fun with smiling people around and that's what I want around me is smiling people. It's contagious, and worth it.

I grew up in Hawaii, and even when I'm back on the mainland you will catch me waving with "shakas" or saying "howzit" when I meet people. I've made it an intentional part of my life because it's fun and different and gives people permission to relax and be themselves around me. And it's also how I see myself, so I'm allowing ME to be true to who I want to be as well.

Chapter 3
CHALLENGING FUN

challenging - adj. testing one's abilities; demanding

One day, my brother Tim called me with a suggestion that led to one of my great discoveries. "Hey Ry, let's do an Ironman 70.3 race!"

Ok, hold on a second. I've always been athletic, I'm a good hiker, and I play soccer regularly. I am a good body surfer and in general a strong waterman. An Ironman 70.3 however, is a different beast altogether. We're talking a 1.2 mile swim with a 56 mile bike ride followed by a half marathon - 13.1 miles. Prior to this conversation I had never run more than 3 miles in a row in my life and I had never ridden a road bicycle. I felt like a decent swimmer, but 30-40 minutes face down in the water had never even crossed my mind. Naturally, I responded with "Sounds like fun! Let's do it!"

We spent some time talking about how amazing it would be, and what kind of a race we were looking for until we settled on Ironman 70.3 in Lake Tahoe, California. I left that conversation pumped, ready to take on the world. When I got home I talked with my wife about the idea, and since she is supremely supportive she said, "Ok, sounds great!"

So, I went online and purchased my ticket. That ticket would start me on a journey of grueling pain, expense and yet another life-changing breakthrough.

It was March of 2015 and the race was September 20th that same year. I had about 6 months to get in good enough shape to survive the day. In my mind though, I wanted to be fast on race day and not merely survive. I felt like this should be easy, so I did what anyone else might do and I procrastinated my training. The idea of having done the race was amazing, but the idea of spending 20 hrs per week slugging out the miles and then actually doing the race? Not so much.

I spent a lot of time looking at gear, and finding just the right running shoes, and triathlon suit. I researched wetsuits, bikes, bike shoes, helmets; the list goes on and on. I had nothing that could be considered a tool to help with either my training OR the race. I didn't own a pair of running shoes or a bike. I didn't even own a pair of goggles! What I did actually own was a pair of speedos because I used to body surf The Wedge in Newport Beach and you kind of need them to survive those waves.

After months had passed, I looked at the calendar and realized that I had 90 days until my race. And what did I have to show for it? I had gone for a few 3 mile runs and made it a point to push myself harder at soccer, but training was definitely not in full swing. I quickly downloaded a guide online titled "Training for Your First Ironman 70.3" and I skipped ahead to the 90-day mark and started there.

Step number one was to learn how to swim. I mean, I knew how to swim but not a freestyle long distance stroke. I had never learned how to swim and breathe at the same time. When body surfing, your head is always up out of the water to see over the waves and chop, or when swimming to catch the wave you're just holding your breath so this was all new to me. I went down to my local lake with my speedos and new goggles and started swimming. After about 150 yards, I was done. I could hardly breathe and I was floating in deep dark scary water. Eventually, I completed my swim across the channel the remaining 150 yards. After much diliberation I swam back the 300 yards in one go, but I was floating on my back like an otter. This was going to take some work.

Over the next 2 weeks, I purchased a gym membership with an olympic-size pool and spent hours watching swim training videos on YouTube. I would go to the pool and swim often twice a day and focused 100% of my training on learning how to swim. I had been watching a method called "swim smooth" out of Australia and the mantra was: slow is smooth and smooth is fast. I focused on my technique and learning how to get my "forever stroke" going. Then, it happened. I completed the 1.2 mile swim in 40 minutes. I felt like I could swim twice as far when that happened, and all of a sudden I felt like this thing was going to be doable.

I mean, if I could complete the swim portion then I could fake it on the bike, right? So I bought a bike on Craigslist for $150 and started riding. As it turns out, riding 56 miles in one go is no joke. On my second ride I destroyed a component on the bike, which as it turned out was not fixable because the bike was so old. This meant Upgrade #1 to a $800 bike that would help me accomplish what I committed to doing when I first paid for my Ironman ticket. The biggest bummer was that it was still going to take 3 weeks to get my parts and if you're following along in the timeline I'm about 80 days away from my race at this point and I hadn't learned how to ride a road bike yet.

While I waited for the parts to arrive I turned to running. I had to be able to run 13.1 miles after I had completed a 1.2 mile swim and a 56 mile bike ride. My current pace was 11:40 minutes per mile for 3.3 miles. For those of you who know running, you're welcome for the chuckle. For those of you who don't know running, a decent half marathon pace is about 8 minutes per mile and a bad pace is about 10 minutes per mile, so at nearly 12 minutes per mile, I wasn't even close.

I stuck to my workout plan and swam twice a week and ran 3 days a week. On the days I was supposed to be biking I would alternate running and swimming. After a few weeks, my parts finally arrived. I hurried down to the bike shop to get them installed and they laughed at me. "We can have it done in about 6 weeks," they said callously.

I begged and pleaded and whined and complained but it didn't matter. They were a bike shop in the middle of summer in a big time biking community and they were slammed with business.

So what did I do? Once again, I turned my attention to

YouTube to learn how to build a bike from nothing more than the frame. I purchased $80 in tools and went to work. Fortunately I'm fairly handy, but even still it took me all weekend to get it functioning correctly: All those gears are really difficult to get lined up. I finished the bike at 1 am on Saturday then woke up at 6 am on Sunday to go for my first ride with the new setup.

Unfortunately, I was a little behind schedule with the biking aspect of things so I had no choice but to punish myself until I was caught up to my training schedule. Six weeks away from the big race, I started training on the bike. Day #1 I had no choice but to ride 30 miles, so I picked a route that I thought I could complete and got to it. After the first 4 miles I felt great, and was loving cycling. Then I came to something called "Heart Rate Ridge" or more aptly nicknamed "Heart Attack Hill."

For a seasoned cyclist this was not much more than good training, but to the uninitiated it was 2 miles of torture straight up. I pushed and gasped, and fought for every inch until I finally crested the summit and saw 6 more miles of hills just like it. I took a slug of hydration liquid from my bottle and soldiered on.

I cleared that section and started the long undulating path to Shasta Dam which is a beautiful ride along a very scenic lake. I made it to the turnaround point 15 miles in and that is when it hit me: I was smiling. I thought back and realized that I had been smiling the whole time. Even when it was painful, I was still smiling. I started to think back to my running and swimming and all the ups and downs of my training to that point and I realized that I LOVED IT!

Don't get me wrong. It was challenging and painful. I had to overcome obstacles and thought patterns. I had to break habits and form new ones. I had to learn more in 6 weeks than I had learned in the last 6 years about pushing my body to my limits and then learning how to push beyond that. I inadvertently painted myself into a corner with my training by procrastinating and yet I was unfazed. I was having a blast training harder than I had ever thought I would need to, and I was enjoying the journey that this ticket had bought me.

HAVING FUN IS A MINDSET

I had learned how to be happy and enjoy life through the struggles. It seems like a miracle thinking about it now, but I know how it happened. When I had my breakthrough moment back in Hawaii, I planted a seed of hope, joy and happiness inside. Over the few years leading up to this moment, I cultivated and watered that seed. I made sure that my goals in life never overshadowed the ultimate outcome, which was to enjoy my life NOW.

This isn't something that came easily or suddenly; it was only the moment of inception that planted the seed. The real work comes from daily choices. When you're trudging to work, you have a decision to make. Water that seed of hope and find the silver lining or bury the seed deeper and reiterate that you hate your job. You come home to a house full of dishes and toys and all you want to do is sit and relax or have a good cry, do you water the seed of joy or feed the depression inside?

There are so many struggles in daily life that it's no wonder that many have trouble finding the joy in it. The kids are fighting and talking back, the bills are piling up, the car just broke down, the list goes on and on and on. That's reality. And in that reality, you have a choice to make. Are you going to live your life or is your life going to live you? One way or the other, you are going to get through it, but will you enjoy the process or will you arrive at the end, battered and beaten?

One of my favorite poems is by Edgar A. Guest, *Don't Quit*. My Grandmother used to have it in her bathroom along with a collection of all our accomplishments and other memorabilia from over the years. I loved to just sit there and look at all the things my family had done, from my grandfather's big invention of the LockRidge tool to my mother's first car. A trip to her bathroom lasted a lot longer than it should have, but one thing I always did was read and memorize this poem:

DON'T QUIT

Edgar A. Guest

When things go wrong, as they sometimes will,
When the road you're trudging seems all uphill,
When the funds are low and the debts are high,
And you want to smile, but you have to sigh,
When care is pressing you down a bit-
Rest if you must, but don't you quit.

Life is queer with its twists and turns,
As every one of us sometimes learns,
And many a fellow turns about
When he might have won had he stuck it out.
Don't give up though the pace seems slow -
You may succeed with another blow.

Often the goal is nearer than
It seems to a faint and faltering man;
Often the struggler has given up
When he might have captured the victor's cup;
And he learned too late when the night came down,
How close he was to the golden crown.

> Success is failure turned inside out -
> The silver tint in the clouds of doubt,
> And you never can tell how close you are,
> It might be near when it seems afar;
> So stick to the fight when you're hardest hit -
> It's when things seem worst that you must not quit

I understand that you will not be able to enjoy every second of your life. If you get in a car accident, you're likely to have some physical pain, more than likely some financial pain, and you will most certainly have some emotional pain. There is nothing fun about that. Your kids will push your buttons. They know where those buttons of annoyance are and how hard they can push them, and they'll do it. It's not fun. There will be moments of struggle that you can't foresee or preempt but ultimately what it all comes down to is how you have cultivated your soul which will determine how you respond to those circumstances.

Start with the small things, and then move up to larger ones as you grow. Let's say the barista gets your drink order wrong at the local coffee shop. You have a bunch of choices: 1- You can chalk it up to syncopation and enjoy whatever drink you ended up with, or 2- you can take it back and find out if they can replace it with the correct drink. 3- You could take it with you and drink it with contempt or worse, 4- throw it out and don't drink it at all.

You could let this mix-up start your day off with proof that it's going to be a bad day, or you could allow it to lead you to a new form of enjoying life. The choice is yours on how you will respond. I'm telling you from experience that it's more difficult in the beginning to find the joy in mistakes. As you grow in having fun and loving life's quirks and experiences the easier it is to just smile through the challenges.

Remember This: Without Challenges You Will Forget How Awesome You Are!

We are all amazing. Some people are better than others at certain things, but most of the time that is only because of passion and habit. It's the challenges that help us discover hidden or unknown abilities, attitudes, and convictions. If you are never challenged, then how do you know how you will respond?

RACE DAY

I completed my training as the program instructed those final 90 days. I did the miles, I put in the work and I was already successful in my mind. Admittedly though, the last few weeks of training were really hard to get up for: I wanted to still have a family when I was done with my race, so I tried to always train on off hours or when people were sleeping. Somehow I completed it though and I felt good.

As a family we decided to make it worth taking a trip to Lake Tahoe prior to my race. It's only about a 4 hour drive from where we live but I definitely needed some time to acclimate because when choosing this race both my brother and I forgot that the lake sits at 6,200ft of elevation, and we live far below that level of elevation. So, we rented a cabin and packed in all the kids, my brother and his wife, and even decided to include grandma and grandpa. During this, my brother Tim and I poked around all of our gear that we brought, planning what we would carry with us and what we would leave at the transitions. The planning itself was a lot of fun for everyone; it made it feel real and close.

The morning of the race arrived to the sound of my alarm clock at 4am, but honestly, I didn't really sleep much the night before anyway. I had to get a good breakfast in me with enough time for it to fully digest prior to the race. I was inspired by Rich Roll and his book Finding Ultra to go all vegan with my training, so my breakfast was a custom blend of oats, almond milk, hemp seeds, chia seeds, flax seeds, banana, cocoa powder, spirulina, and whatever else suited my fancy that morning. I finished that, packed up the truck and my Dad drove us down to the staging area.

The time passed slowly and quickly at the same time if that's even possible, but once it was time to enter what they call the race shoot, I knew it was game on. The cannon boomed, then GO, GO, GO!

The race started with a running splash through the cold water with thousands of other athletes until you get to swim depth, then a dive into the frigid lake and we all started swimming. No matter how much training you have, nothing prepares you for being mauled by 100's of people while trying to calmly swim your stroke to complete a 1.2 mile swim. Bang! Right at the beginning I got kicked square in the face and my goggles started leaking. Finally after about 10 minutes of swimming I came to clear water as the rest of the participants all found their place swimming the lake.

The swim portion was easily my favorite leg of the race even despite the challenges it provided. When I rounded the last buoy and headed down the final stretch towards the exit and transition area I could feel my strength growing. I punched it, and doubled my pace. I began to pass dozens of other swimmers. I found out later that I exited the water in 33rd place which blew me away. I have pictures taken of me coming out of the water with a huge grin from ear to ear.

I quickly ran to my gear bag, stripped off my wetsuit and found my bike out of a sea of carbon ponies. As I started to ride I began to sing, adrenalin pumping away through me after that incredible swim. I was feeling so good, I actually began to worship. Out loud. I couldn't help it. I had to express how much joy was inside of me. I could see on the faces of many of the cyclists that I began to pass that they were annoyed by it, but I couldn't have cared less. I was elated and it was going to come out loud and proud.

For the next 40 miles I rode hard and passed many riders and was also passed by many riders. I could quickly see where my lack of experience showed, but I could also see where my training paid off. Then came the self-named "hill of death." I'm pretty sure I was passed by a thousand people on this hill.

I found out in the middle of this torture test the reality that a 215 pound man is harder to move up a big hill than a 90 pound woman; it's simply physics. This hill was 6.5 miles straight up to 8,200ft of elevation from about 6,500ft.

There is a picture of me on the bike during that hill, and I'm smiling and throwing a shaka to the camera. I couldn't help it. It was hard work, but the joy of the accomplishment was overwhelming. When I finally crested that hill and headed down the 3.5 mile descent, physics worked in my favor. I was pushing 50 mph on a 1" tire with nothing more than spandex and a plastic helmet to keep me safe.

My legs were trashed at this point, and I was in a ton of pain and I still had 16 miles to ride before I could start my half marathon. Those miles went fairly quick, and it wasn't until maybe 2 miles left that the smile finally faded from my face.

Then the payoff...

I rounded the last curve and there was my whole family cheering, "Go Daddy!!!" I could barely hold back my tears. They had sat there for hours waiting for me to come riding in and when I did, they were jumping all over the place and shouting for me. If I didn't have to keep my focus I would have definitely stopped and joined in with them! I started crying for joy as I pushed on.

After about 2 hrs on the bike it felt very strange to transition to running. I swapped my shoes and changed my helmet for a hat and started running. The first aid station came very quickly and it was a good thing too: I needed food and water and a masseuse. About 1 mile into my 13.1 mile run, bang, my left knee went out on me; I collapsed onto the pavement. Rubbing my knee and testing it for strength I determined that I could stand up and even start limp-running a bit. I had come this far, so I soldiered on.

Three miles later, bang! My right knee went out on me and down I went again. This one was hard to overcome. I still had 9 miles to go and I knew I had just enough to make it, if my knees were in shape. I started to contemplate, calling the race done. I had made a strong showing and no one would fault me for dropping out at this point. Then, I thought about my kids waiting at the finish line for a dad that would never come. That brief image is all that it took. Oh, forget that! I immediately changed the image to crossing the line, which meant that I'm getting my ass up and they are going to have to drag me off this course before I quit!

As I limped on, the pain was almost unbearable. I kept thinking about my kids waitint at the finishline for their dad who may never show up. I thought about my oldest son Ezekiel when he used to play football at 7 and 8 years old. It was very cute but he was one of the smallest kids on the field. Yet, his first year of football he started as a defensive end because he wouldn't quit. He would push hard and continue on until the other kid gave up and then he would make the play. At the end of the season, he was given the "Rudy" award for the kid with the biggest heart.

So, during my time of pain and struggle all I kept saying to myself was, "Ezekiel wouldn't quit." Over and over again, "Ezekiel wouldn't quit, Ezekiel wouldn't quit. You can't give up, you can't give them permission to quit when things get hard." Time started to pass and I was making a little headway.

I had pulled myself from the pit of self pity and continued on with my plan: run the downhills, limp-jog the flats, and walk the uphills. Once I got my focus back on finishing the race I started to see all of these amazingly inspirational athletes around me. I talked with many of them as we ran together. Sometimes we would pass each other then catch back up again later, checking in to see how the other person was doing. I may not have known them prior to the race, but there's an undeniable bond that occurs when people are going through the same experience with together; especially when they are clearly also in pain. Yet, they keep going; so I do as well.

Then came the last push to the finish line. I could see it about ½ mile ahead of me. This overwhelming sense of pride and accomplishment welled up inside of me and I felt a wave of adrenaline hit me again as I started running up the huge hill to the top of the main Olympic Village from the 1960 Winter Olympics. As I rounded the last corner, I could hear the announcer calling my as I crossed the finish line.

I Did It

I finished with hands held high and the cheers of the crowd, but it was the squeals of my children and the loving cheers of my wife that cut through the all the noise. My final time was clocked in at 7:52:38. Seven hours, fifty two minutes and thirty eight seconds of sheer pain, and bliss all at the same time.

The challenge gave me a sense of myself that I had never known before. I AM good enough. I have what it takes. I am a good father and husband. I am a good brother and son, and I have the ability to do anything that I put my mind to. Even when finishing seems out of reach, I know that I can push beyond what my body tells me I can do. I earned a level of mental toughness that is impossible to get without being challenged first.

Never give in, never give in, never, never,

> never, never - in nothing, great or small, large or petty - never give in except to convictions of honour and good sense.
>
> *-Winston Churchill*

Not everything that you attempt in your life will be easy and free from challenges. It's only how you respond to those challenges and what you derive from them that will determine the level of happiness that you feel. It's not always fun in the process, and it's not always fun in the outcome but when enjoying life is a top priority you will have the inner fortitude to push through it and come out on the other side greater than you started.

Begin right now to cultivate a core value for fun and the enjoyment of life. Start with the small things and build up to the bigger things. This way, when you are faced with a challenge that is really hard and you're not sure that you can overcome it, you will have something to hold on to. You will have peace of mind that the outcome, even if it's not fun in the moment, is part of the process of life and that you will be ok.

I've found that achieving a goal without having enjoyed the journey is hardly worth the accomplishment. Take the time to allow the beautiful things of life to fill your soul. There is always a silver lining in every challenge, and in some cases the challenge itself is the silver lining.

IRONMAN® 70.3 LAKE TAHOE 2015

Always smiling, I couldn't wipe the grin off my face the whole time. Even while in pain, I was still having a crazy amount of fun! It was hard, really hard, and there were times I thought about quitting, but it never took away from my experinece. That's the power of having fun!

After a 1.2 mile swim   Taken @ mile 40 half way up the Hill-O-Death   Finishing the Race 70.3 Miles, 2 trashed knees

I've had some people ask me if I have any triathlon training or materials so I started a group. when training for my next race I share tips, tricks, struggles, and successes. If you're interested in doing a triathlon, or just want to be on the list to get those emails, you can join the group here.

www.ryan8.com/triathlons

Chapter 4
PRIORITIZE FUN

prioritize - verb. determine the order for dealing with a series of items or tasks according to their relative importance

This morning my youngest son pulled all the books off the bookshelf then peed all over them. Yes, that's right. He peed all over our books. As you can easily imagine, I was very upset. Throwing a tantrum like a child, I tossed the pee-soaked books back on the ground after picking them up and discovering they were wet and it wasn't from water. I sent him to time-out and fumed about my ruined books for a few minutes.

After calming down and allowing the emotions to process all the way through, I fetched him from time-out, helped HIM clean up the pee and made him put the books away. That's right: a 2 year old cleaned up after himself, and he did a great job.

A few minutes after all that, I just had to laugh about it. Being a parent is fun. You never know what your kid is going to do or say next. The story that I now have because of dealing with this in a proper way will bring me endless joy; especially when I tell the story to one of his future girlfriends.

I love all my kids so much and they are so cool. Each one has their own personality and each one comes at life from a different perspective. It's so much fun. Yet, sometimes there is a clash in ideals. It's inevitable, actually. I prefer to read my books unsoiled, Micah on the other hand had a little accident but thought it was fun to watch his pee fly all over the place.

Already telling this story has brought me more joy and love for my son. It makes me want to do amazing things for him and with him, though I draw the line at another peeing fest on books. Participating in activities with my children draws me into their world so I can remember what it's like to be a kid again. Parenting is supposed to be fun.

The difference between being upset all day long, and learning how to transition my emotions from irritation to amusement comes from choosing to have fun being a dad. The priority for me is to enjoy the process of raising my kids, and that means that when the negative emotions come to the surface, I will actively chose a different emotion. It takes a little practice to shift a perspective from one form to the other but the key behind it is prioritizing the things that are most important.

When my son had fun all over my books, it was easy to be upset. That was the default emotion. He didn't do it to upset me though. He was just trying to have fun. His focus was not on me and what might upset me or make me happy. The books came out of the shelves in a way that was fascinating, so he kept doing it. At some point he felt the "urge" and let-er-rip. At that point, a new game was made called lets see what happens next.

To a child, they have their priorities mostly straight. Fun is at the top. Playing is a priority. Keeping dad's books in crisp condition is very low on the list. What he learned from our interaction was that dad doesn't like me to ruin his stuff. So the priority for loving me moved up on his list. And that is the key to enjoying life, getting priorities in the proper order.

WORK HARD

I have been trained since I was small to work really hard, or at least try really hard. I have been told that if I'm not succeeding, then I need to work harder and put in more time. In school, that means studying harder while at work that means putting in extra hours. At home that means less sleep in order to get these other tasks completed.

The goal of course is to be successful, happy or free from struggles that hold us back. I was trained to forgo short term rewards for the BIGGER PICTURE. Society dictates that if we save and store, and work hard: you know, the whole, "you can rest when you're dead" kind of attitude is praised and employable. And yet, it feels empty. We work so hard to have fun that when we get there, we don't know how to relax.

BAD PARADIGM:
Work + Work + Work X 50 years = Success

The philosophy to "Deny your wants and focus on your needs, unless you get lucky and make a bunch of money early on then teach me how you did it" is the order of the day, but I'm here to tell you that this is completely backwards!

The same is expected for parenting: "Pour your life into your kids and deny your own dreams and sacrifice all relationships for the sake of the kids. Put their happiness and success above your relationship with your spouse and friends." This way of thinking sounds more like a recipe for divorce and unhappy kids.

GOOD PARADIGM:
Passion + Habit = Success

We need to find our passion, follow it and discover how we can make our dreams a reality all while having fun. Find work that we enjoy because we're going to be more successful at it anyway, and when it's all said and done we will have a life worthy of reflecting on with a smile.

Imagine this: there's a championship game on the line with your favorite sports team. The coach goes into the locker room and sits the athletes down. He gives a big motivating speech that brings resolute tears to the player's eyes. As the underdogs, the team they are facing are the reigning champions and should win this game. So, what does he say?

"You've worked hard. You've given me everything I've asked of you. You have prepared for this moment your entire lives. You all have what it takes to beat this team, and I know that if you work together we can win! Now go out there and have some fun!"

It's always the same. Go have fun. Get out there and do your best but make sure you are having fun. Why?

It's because all the hard work isn't for some silly medal of achievement. We start doing something because you enjoy it. We want to be the best at something because it is FUN. Once we achieve a high level of performance there is nothing left but to enjoy being the best.

Having recently taken up triathlons I found out that when a participant completes a triathlon, regardless of whether he or she is first or last, they give them a finisher medal. One writer of a blog that I read the other day talked about how he doesn't keep his medals. He wrote about how himself and other racers actually hate that medals are given out to everyone. I WAS SHOCKED! I love my medals. I hang them proudly in my office and every one of them reminds me of what it took to even complete the race. A Half Ironman is a Double Olympic Triathlon, 70.3 miles in total. For me, if an athlete can complete 70.3 miles in under 8 hours then they deserve a medal of achievement.

When I look at my medals or someone asks me about them,

I am overwhelmed with pride and happiness. I am proud of what it took to achieve the medal. I am reminded of the days surrounding the race, and the circumstances leading up to it. I remember the training calls with my brother, and the joy that I shared with my family.

The difference between my outlook and the writer of the blog is the goal vs the journey. The medals remind me of what it took to accomplish them and of how much fun I had during the race. They bring back good memories of the journey. Yet, for the blog writer who doesn't keep his medals, they remind him of losing. They are a reminder that he wasn't good enough, and of the goal that he failed to achieve.

The goal for me was to do something amazing, and to have fun while doing it. I took my training seriously but not so serious that I forgot why I bothered trying to do it in the first place. It's true for sports, and it's true for other areas of our life as well. Prioritize having fun in the process of whatever it is that you are trying to accomplish and you are more likely to be successful when you're done.

PRIORITIES

No matter what we're trying to accomplish, we have a measurable set of priorities. Whether we write them down or not, we all have a set of rules that we live by.

For me, the #1 priority is my **time**. We all get the same amount of time every day and what I do with mine is precious to me. For instance, I don't like it when clients waste my time. You know the kind: they talk for 45 minutes about something that can be resolved in 4 minutes after reading an email. I don't mind though when someone at the local coffee shop, for example, interrupts my day to talk briefly, because that highlights my #2 priority, **people**.

There is a parable in the *Bible* that was a mystery to me for 20 years until one day it clicked.

> A bad manager was found out by his boss that he was doing a bad job and was about to be fired. He thought to himself, "What am I going to do? I can't do physical labor and I don't have any other skills…"

> He reasoned that if he helps out the people who owe his boss money that when he is fired he can get a job with one of those guys. So he goes to each one and says, if you will pay back ½ of what you owe I'll mark that you paid in full.

> When the boss got back from his trip he found out what the manager had done. Much to his surprise the master praised him for being so shrewd. The boss tells him "good job, you finally get the point."

Now, this doesn't seem like a very Biblical story and it baffled me for a long time. Until one day, it all clicked: it's all about people. The steward knew that by taking care of people, his life would be taken care of. There is value in taking care of others the way you would want to be treated. There is value in making people a priority in your dealings because as you take care of them, they will take care of you. The next time you need a good deal, or ask for a referral, they will gladly share with you. People are not dollar signs and when you treat them with respect and in a generous caring way they will reciprocate. Since you reap what you sow, people will treat you with the same value that you show them.

The master in this story will have his business grow because of what the manager had done. And now the manager is well liked in the community and will be more likely to get a better deal for future business transactions. Shrewd indeed!

PRIORITY #3 HAVE FUN!!!

Making fun a priority does not mean that it has to be the top priority; it just means that it needs to be on your priority list and preferably high on your priority list. When I'm training for a triathlon it get's bumped down below commitment because not all training is fun. When I was at the Ironman race however, it went right up to the top of the list because for me all that hard work was so I could have fun when I participated in the event. And as you read in chapter 3, I had a blast!

You've heard it said and possibly said it yourself, "Work Hard. Play Hard." There are times in my own life when I've taken a vacation because I needed a little relaxation. Only when I get there I needed more than relaxation. I needed to have some fun!

I know for myself that when I'm not having fun doing something, it takes longer than it should to complete, it will be emotionally draining, and I'll likely not do as good of a job.

I apply this same principal to parenting, eating healthy, and my relationship with my wife.

I recommend that you take a time to write down your current priorities for some areas of your life. Be honest. If fun isn't at the top of the list or at least high up there, conscientiously move it up the list.

THE RESEARCH

There have been many studies on how having fun relates to higher overall performance. If you Google "best companies to work for," you will get hundreds of results by the top names in business journalism. On those lists are always some kind of a "Fun" factor. Either in the culture that the companies create or in the philosophy that a happy employee is a good employee.

Google actually tops most lists when it comes to corporate environment and employees being happy to go to work. Trader Joe's tell their employees to talk to each other about their day while they are working. They are encouraged to engage with customers as their friends and they are told to have fun. Zappos is known for having a fun working environment; they go so far as to allow their employees to choose their own managers and negotiate their own pay.

I read an article in Forbes titled "Happy Employees = Hefty Profits" where they talked about the top 5 things that make for happy employees.

1) Pay fairly

2) Deliver awesome benefits.

3) Keep an open leadership door

4) Share the profits.

5) Make your workplace fun.

In fact, every article I could find about happy employees and high performance listed having fun on some level.

Mark Twain wrote, "The human race has only one really effective weapon, and that is laughter. The moment it arises, all our hardnesses yield, all our irritations and resentments slip away and a sunny spirit takes their place."

If you type "contagious laughter subway" into YouTube, you'll find that there are some people who do experiments where they get on a train and start laughing, where within a few minutes the entire train is cracking up and no one has a clue why. Try watching "happy chewbacca" without cracking a smile...I can't even say it without smiling.

HERE ARE SOME WAYS HAVING FUN IMPROVES YOUR LIFE

Fun breaks up boredom. There is actually a scale to measure boredom called the Boredom Proneness Scale (BPS). Yes, it's real. They have linked being bored to higher stress, depression, and addiction.

This study showed a 5% drop in overall brain activity. It also showed that despite the drop there was increased levels in the areas of the brain that contemplate one's own life. Even to the point of making up hypothetical events and thinking negatively about others.

In layman's terms, when you are bored, you start thinking about stuff that doesn't exist and you create scenarios that never happened.

What triggers boredom may come down to dopamine. Dopamine is what your body produces when you get a hug, or are rewarded for behavior. When you suffer from chronic boredom you actually get a reduced level of dopamine receptors in your brain and get reduced capacity to benefit from being praised for doing well.

If you spend too much time bored, when you do have fun it isn't that fun. I see this with my kids when they need a rest day and spend too much time sitting in front of the TV. Even getting them to get up and go to the park or go get ice cream is like pulling teeth. Once we get out the door it takes awhile for them to get into it. It's always the same, but eventually they will get with the program and start having fun.

Boredom is a natural trigger that reminds us that we are not actively living our lives. It doesn't come from being relaxed. It only comes from having the energy to complete something but it's either out of our control like waiting in a doctor's office, or it's tedious and uninteresting. Whatever the cause, prolonged exposure to boredom actually will lead to depression.

Fun Reduces Stress. We all have a working relationship with stress. We know what it is, and we know how it makes us feel but here are a few things you may not know about how stress impacts your physical body.

Stress ignites the fight or flight response in your brain. If you're a fighter (like me) or a flighter it will be greatly increased during times of stress. In your brain it releases cortisol and adrenaline. These are good things when you are trying to avoid being eaten by a bear but not so much when it's time to complete that TPS report or when you're trying to get your kids to bed. It's also not so good for the latest diet trend or to try to handle stress permanently.

Symptoms of chronic stress include: depression, irritability, anxiety, headaches & insomnia. Chronic stress is a factor in behaviors like overeating or not eating enough, alcohol or drug abuse, or social withdrawal.

Stress hormones affect your heart and blood pressure. What's the first thing the doc says when someone goes in for a heart problem? Reduce stress in your life. For women it can trigger premenopausal symptoms.

When you're under stress the liver produces extra sugars to help you have the energy to overcome the reason for the stress. It's impossible to eliminate all stress from our lives, and sometimes stress can bring positive results as it kicks us into gear to go a little further than what our comfort level allows. Unfortunately, if you're body doesn't use those sugars up when remaining in a continual state of stress it leads to a bunch of health problems. Heartburn, acid reflux, ulcers are the common ones that we know about but it also causes other problems like nausea, vomiting, dietary issues like diabetes, Crohn's disease and gluten intolerance.

Unresolved stress also causes problems with sex. For men, it can cause impotence and lowered sperm production. For women, it can cause painful or irregular cycles along with early menopause. For women it also reduces the desire for sex.

And finally, when our body remains in a constant state of stress, it suppresses the immune system and causes weight gain. When faced with danger, your body needs all the energy it can to go to the muscles so you can perform at a higher level. One of the things that causes this is that other parts of the body need to slow down for a bit to conserve energy. Under prolonged or chronic stress your body creates cortisol which causes reduced immune system, and weight gain.

Fun Fulfills Social Needs. According to Maslow's Hierarchy of Needs social interactions are a right above the basics of food, water, and security. One example of this is that women statistically live longer than men. In long term marriages if the wife dies first, typically the man will go shortly after even if he was healthy. Conversely, if the husband dies first, it is likely the wife will continue on long after. Why do we continue to see these statistics? This is because women are generally more social and have the ability to create a natural support group for themselves and deal with the loss through support.

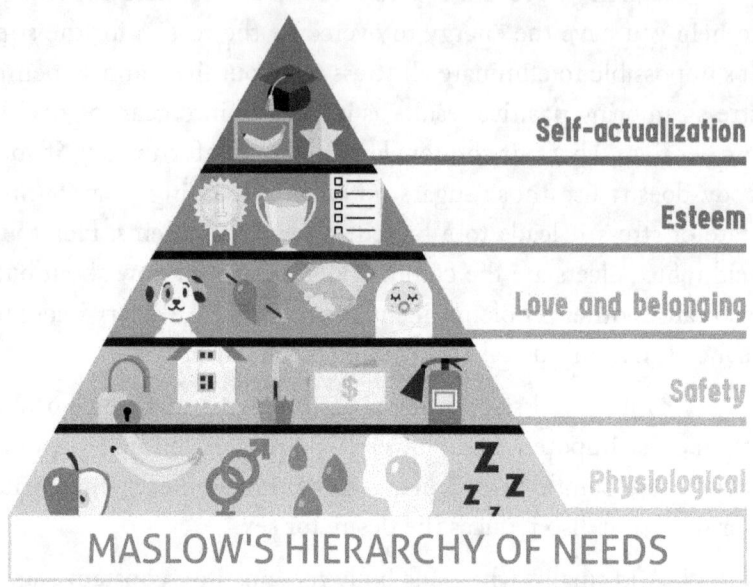

As you can see from Maslow's chart love and belonging are one of the top elements of human needs. When we are having fun it's usually with other people. Or if we did it on our own, we relate the story to others, causing all those happy body chemicals to be released. Having fun is a human NEED, not a human want.

AN INTERESTING STUDY ABOUT MONEY AND HAPPINESS

Amit Kumar - PhD from Cornell University, has made his area of study around spending money and happiness. He found that money spent on doing increases happiness vs money spent on having, which doesn't add to happiness at all and can actually reduce overall happiness.

"Psychological research has shown that experiential purchases (a hike in the woods; a trip to Rome) bring more happiness than material purchases (a designer shirt; a flat-screen television)."

"...people talk more about their experiences than their possessions and derive more value from doing so."

"I have investigated how experiential purchases promote enhanced anticipatory pleasure, provide hedonic benefits through utility derived from storytelling, and also have downstream consequences in terms of fostering social connectedness and prosocial behavior."

Quotes used from - www.kumar-amit.com

In his research he found that the reason experiential purchases added to overall life enjoyment is because they create storytelling opportunities. He noted that when people tell the story of their adventures, it satisfies a basic human need to be social. His studies have shown that the story is the differing component. People will talk about the stuff that they bought, but it doesn't provide the same effect as the experience they just had. If you need to make a purchase, start thinking about what story you are going to tell or create by purchasing that thing. Even a *preemptive* story can be satisfying in small doses.

So can money buy you happiness...no. But using our resources to have fun and enjoy our life does create happiness. Relating the story to our friends and family creates happiness. And it strengthens bonds and creates joy.

PUTTING IT ALL TOGETHER

We all know that life without fun in it is not a life that we want to live. I think that the challenge is in the daily grind. There are so many things which steal our fun that it's difficult to keep it all in the proper perspective.

Take for example the story about my son peeing on the books: It's funny now, and probably hilarious to those of you who have similar stories. In the moment, however, it was not fun. It was quite disgusting, and brought up something about me that I needed to take a look at in regards to my anger. Why did I care so much about these books that I would probably never read again?

Because I have chosen to make fun a priority in my life, in all areas of my life. I was able to LOVE on my son and let him know that it's ok that we make mistakes as long as we take responsibility for them and clean up the mess after. (Yeah, I said that to a 2 year old but he gets it. Young children are much smarter than people give them credit for.)

I was able to help him clean up the mess with compassion for the task at hand. Trying to put books back on a shelf for a toddler is a momentous undertaking. I was able to show him my love and my pain at the same time. He learned about compassion and responsibility.

All of that occurred because I chose to have fun being a dad. Even if that means that I clean up pee pee books from time to time.

Having fun doesn't mean you shirk responsibilities, and it doesn't mean that you do whatever you want to do. It just means that in the process of doing what you need to do, make sure that you can do it with a smile or at least a smile at the end.

6 WAYS TO BE PRODUCTIVE AND STILL HAVE FUN

1. Set Various Types of Goals

Goal setting is really a requirement if you want to achieve anything. If you don't know where you are going then how can you be upset when you get somewhere that you don't want to be? Make a plan and follow it. BUT, this surefire way of production is also kind of boring.

> **Here are some example goals:**
> Earn $10,000 per Month
> Write a Book
> Take a Vacation to Italy
> Learn to Play the Guitar
> Climb Mt. Kilimanjaro
> Run a Marathon
> Get Your Degree

All those goals are great, and we know that if we create steps to achieve them then we are likely to get there eventually. Here's where having fun can actually help us achieve our goals better.

Let's start with the financial goal. If we set daily goals that are more like games, we are more likely to actually do them. For example, let's say that one of our action steps is to make 50 cold calls per day. That's a tough pill to swallow. But, it's something worth doing if we make it a game like: for every 10 "No's" we put on a song and dance around. We're going to get through those calls quickly. Perhaps a treat is your motivator, and you're going to reward yourself with a hot fudge sundae after the call. This method isn't just limited to financial goals, but any goal that you make. Whatever it is, if you make mini goals into games you are more likely to get it done.

For a guy that doesn't like to run I had to come up with fun goals to help me get through the training. So, I did this when training for Ironman. I would pick out a tree in the distance and set that as a marker of achievement. Or I would have a fun thing planned for after my run like stopping to get a donut. It didn't matter much what I chose to do, but creating various types of goals made the training fun and I was more successful at it than just slugging out the miles.

Whatever your 5 year, 10 year or life goals are, make a plan and create various fun goals that will help you achieve them quicker.

2. Enjoy The Process

This is actually one of the greatest tips I can give someone in regards to being productive and also enjoying what they are trying to accomplish. ENJOY THE PROCESS!

I'll never forget the second time I climbed Mt. Whitney and how it transformed my life. The first time I climbed the mountain I was with my Dad and we took a 4 day backpacking trip through the backcountry to get there. It was the long way and incidentally it was also the hard way, yet I thoroughly enjoyed it.

The second time though was a 1 day up and back attempt of the summit; a 23 mile round trip starting at 8,500ft elevation. We left at midnight and hiked in the moonlight, which was amazing. What happened to me though was I was so focused on getting to the top that I missed the whole trail. It was dark for most of the trip to the top and by the time I reached the summit and headed back down I was in a hurry to get off the mountain.

I had completely missed out on the journey just to achieve the goal. This is when I realized that the *purpose of a goal is to create a journey*. Here I had missed out on the beauty and splendor of this amazing trail to the top of the highest mountain in the lower 48 states because I was so concerned with getting to the top and back.

The power of that journey I have been able to enjoy later because of my new found appreciation for the journey I was on but during the trip and even the short period of time surrounding it was a total blur. Set a goal, but enjoy the journey!

3. Value Consistency

Every successful journey forms a rhythm. What do I mean by this? Without rhythm we have chaos because no one is bringing in any other contribution. We're all doing the same thing, at the same pace, and even though it's all the same, there's also no consistency in showing forth any growth. If we are not consistent in life then we will have the same results.

There is something so simple and wonderful about being consistent. If you want to be a writer, write everyday no matter what. If you want to run a marathon, get a running plan and stick to it. If you want to learn a new skill be consistent in your training. And if you want to be successful, find ways to stay consistent.

The world will throw things at you and you will get the unexpected in your life. Creating a proper rhythm will be key to enjoying the syncopation that we discussed earlier in this book.

I saw this in my own life with my daughter. She's an amazing girl. She is always having fun and running around the house like crazy. And so, for some reason, it's difficult for her to get ready for school, regardless of how long she has to do it.

One day we were at a Parent/Teacher Conference and we were handed a morning checklist for the kids. I showed it to her and asked if she thought this would help her. When we got home she was so excited about it that we had to tape it up on her closet door immediately. She was never late for school again.

All it took was a small visual reminder to get her back on track to enjoy her journey of childhood. Place a value on consistency, and embrace life's rhythm. Use tools if necessary, but always keep room to roll with the unexpected. Which brings me to our next point.

4. Mix It Up

Just as we need consistency to have fun in the process, we also need to mix it up. If your morning routine is to have a cup of coffee at a specific time, you don't have to change that to mix things up. What you can do is buy a variety of different coffees and give yourself something new to try while still maintaining your consistency.

Think of it as syncopation for your subconscious: You are planning it so it's not like you're being unexpected. But your brain might be expecting one flavor and end up with something completely different, which shakes the routine up. You could also get really crazy and have a cup of tea instead.

All areas of your life will benefit from mixing it up a bit. Studies have shown that once you have mastered something, it gets boring. Let's imagine that you are really great at your job. You're so good in fact that you don't even want to do it anymore. Congratulations! You have made it to "mastery" level. So what do you do? Most people quit, or change companies, or do something to rock their world. That is unnecessary.

It's possible that all you need is to mix things up a bit. Change your focus to another area of growth that you're not as familiar with, or begin to leverage your new found mastery to create new profit centers.

Whatever you are trying to accomplish, if you mix things up while maintaining rhythm you are likely to have fun doing it.

5. Rest

Life is proof that we need rest; you go to sleep every night. If you don't get enough sleep how do you feel the next day? If you go on no sleep for too long you start to lose your mind. For my wife and me, every new baby we had was a torture test in lack of sleep. No one knows what tired is until you have a newborn. If you don't have kids yet, don't even consider arguing your point about being tired studying for finals or any other example. Three to four hours of sleep every night for 6 months straight….yes, that's tired.

Since we know what it's like to be tired physically, and mentally then why oh why do we forget to rest when it comes to being productive? Let's take another example.

It's 3:30 in the afternoon on a Thursday; how focused are you? Most of us could use a nap at that point. Some countries actually do take a nap called a siesta and the British have tea time. The point is that for the next 1 ½ hours our productivity will be very poor. More than likely we will slip into tactics to avoid doing work and choose distractions like social media as a break, but really you are being paid to surf Facebook.

For me, I learned not to fight it. I like to start work earlier around 7:30-8 depending on how I feel that day. I'm most creative in the morning so I will do my creativity items first like writing. By lunch I've accomplished quite a bit.

I like to exercise or do something fun for lunch. I used to take an hour and a half to play pickup basketball or soccer. Currently I like to swim or go for a run, but I prefer to do something FUN during my lunch break. Eating takes about 15 minutes, so I can do that when I'm done.

I get back to work about 1:30 and I work hard until 4pm, which is when I typically end my work day so I can spend the rest of the afternoon and evening with my family. But there are those times when I have a pressing project, in which I know that I'll be spinning my wheels for the next 2 hours if I try to push through it, so I'll take a little extra time learning or growing.

Even during this final push, taking this extra time to read a book or watch YouTube videos, gives my mind a REST for 30 minutes to an hour so I can accomplish my goal. Then I can get back to focus and work until 6:30 if I need to.

Understand though that you are not doing yourself or anyone else a favor by doing your task without the proper rest. Take a day off in the middle of the week if you have to, and you will find that when you come back you will be way more productive than trying to just fight through it slowly.

6. Quality Over Quantity

In high school I learned to order from the $1 menu, mostly because it was cheaper for the quantity I was getting. Later on I realized that I was still spending four or five bucks anyway and I was eating way too much food. One day I decided to order the most expensive burger on the menu for about six dollars. It was delicious and I remained full, and also realized that I saved myself 1000 calories from consuming all of those cheap fillers from the value menu. Just like that, I learned the value of quality over quantity.

If you're a dad, I'm going to help you with this as well. Quality time is not quantity time. It doesn't matter if you're sitting in the same room with your kids. They want the interaction time. Let's say you come home from work at 5pm every day and you spend the rest of your evening in front of a TV and your kids are in the same room with you. That is NOT quality time; that is quantity time. I know people who complain about their Dad's being absent from their entire childhood yet they were always "there" in the home. Being present is more than just being around.

In business we call this quality time as being productive.

It doesn't matter if you work 80hrs per week or 30hrs per week. What matters is what is accomplished. I know sales people that work 60hrs a week and they are barely making ends meet. And I know sales people that work 35hrs per week and are very successful. The difference is simply Quality of work vs Quantity of work.

Here's another kicker for you: the quality stuff is better. Quality time is more fun, quality food is more enjoyable, and quality work will be received better. It's just a fact that when something is quality it is enjoyed more. If you start making fun a priority in your everyday life you will see an increase in your quality.

A chef that loves cooking and food will make better food. A designer that loves what they are designing will create a better product. A mom that has fun playing with her kids will have happier and more enjoyable children. It's really true that when you LOVE what you do, you do better at it and see better results. If that isn't a good argument for making fun a priority then I don't know what is!

We need to start right now to create ways for us to enjoy our life. It's more than just taking vacations and picking up new hobbies. Find ways to make the daily routine fun. Create tools to help us enjoy the processes and set goals that can really get a person excited.

Life is a gift, and it's worth living well.

Chapter 5
EMPOWERING FUN

empower - vb. make (someone) stronger and more confident, especially in controlling their life and claiming their rights

There I was staring at the bottom of an empty box of cinnamon buns and I had one thought on my mind, "What did I just do?". It wasn't the first time, but this particular incident rocked my world.

The story begins when one day my wife told me we were out of diapers and we needed one for when the baby wakes up in the morning. So at 11pm I went out to the store to get diapers. I have 4 kids, so I'm used to these late night trips.

I had developed a reward program for when I had to go out late to do things like this: I bought a treat. This time I wanted a cinnamon bun, but there weren't any singles available. All they had was a full tray of them. I thought about it for a few moments then rushed home with the diapers and my treasure.

On the way home I pounded down 2 of them. I figured that I would save the rest as a treat for the kids the next day. When I got home, all of the lights were off and everyone was asleep, so I plopped down in front of the TV and promptly ate 2 more. After a little while longer I had a few more, and before I knew it there were only 3 left.

I figured I had to destroy the evidence so I headed to the kitchen to throw them out. Instead I ate the rest and then took the box out to the big trash can. When I got back inside, it hit me like a ton of bricks… what had I done?! I knew right then and there that I had a food addiction problem, and it's a bad one. I was up to about

260 lbs during this time but I had been bigger. My wife has never been more than a few pounds over weight and that was when she was pregnant. I felt awful inside and out.

In the morning, while I related to my wife what I had done I was full of shame and embarrassment. I hung my head and told her like I had just done something really bad. I said, "I have a problem and I think I need help." In my mind I was thinking about counseling and possibly a fat camp. I couldn't kick this weight thing and really it was the food addiction that was a real problem. I was stuck in a downward spiral of shame, guilt and fear.

I never expected what happened next and her response was the best gift I've ever received: she laughed. Not a mocking laugh, and not a judgmental laugh. She wasn't laughing out of embarrassment or anything negative. Her gentle, caring laugh told me, "It's not a big deal. You are a powerful man and you can stop if you want to." Her response conveyed, "I love you no matter what and I will help you however you need." Then she asked, "What do you want to do?"

I decided to go on a juicing fast and reboot my system. We were healthy eaters, and most of the time I ate really healthy I just couldn't stop eating. And, when I was out of the house I packed away the junk food.

Ultimately I lost close to 50 lbs and I've kept it off for years now. I had broken free from the shame and power of my weight problem once and for all. I was finally free from my addiction.

The reason the laugh was so valuable to me is because it took something that I saw as a huge deal: a giant mountain to climb or a vast ocean to swim and turned it into a simple thing to overcome. It was the power of fun.

There were days that I struggled, but I made my journey one of excitement and having fun. I ended up enjoying my weight loss journey so much that when I set out to just kill my sweet tooth I ended up a picture of health all because of the simplicity of enjoying life.

EMPOWERING

There is nothing more empowering than to know that my life has been approved by God. When I realized this, I was able to stop seeking approval from my Mom, Dad, Sister, Brother, Boss, Social Media, etc... I was free to live the life that I want. What it did for my marriage, learning how to enjoy life with my wife, was an amazing breakthrough.

One of my great discoveries along my path to enjoying life is this ancient proverb:

> "Go then, eat your bread in happiness and drink your wine with a cheerful heart; for God has already approved your works. Let your clothes be white all the time, and let not oil be lacking on your head. Enjoy life with the woman whom you love all the days of your fleeting life which He has given to you under the sun; for this is your reward in life and in your toil in which you have labored under the sun."
>
> *- King Solomon*

My eyes were opened up to the truth about life. It's not the things we did or the jobs we had in this life which echo into eternity; it's the connections that we make and the example we leave behind that will be remembered. Choosing to live a life of happiness and fulfillment is the greatest way to impact those around us and future generations.

When I do things that hurt me and my life, it's wasting the gift. If I want to go out and get drunk every night we all know how that will end. Is that behavior worthy of approval? Of course not, but who I am is worthy of approval. The natural consequence of the behavior will speak for itself and I will pay the consequences physically.

The opposite is also true. If I work 50, 60, 70 hours per week then I will also pay for that behavior. Sure, it seems responsible to be a hard diligent worker but it's really missing out on the big picture. I will likely be successful with money and possibly my career but most of the other areas of my life will suffer. My wife and kids wouldn't be happy with me, and my health will probably suffer as well.

We work hard and sacrifice so we can enjoy our lives and our family. Ask any kid if they would rather have an Xbox or their dad home more often. With few exceptions, they will say they want their dad home more. Ideally they probably want both, but dad is definitely first priority. The purpose of a life well lived is so we don't miss out on our life.

One of the great Robin Williams movies, Hook, portrays a workaholic lawyer who is missing out on his kids baseball games, school plays and other big moments in the pursuit of providing. As a father myself, it's no surprise to me to see that the main plot shows how in the process of trying to rescue them, he had forgotten how to have fun.

I love how in the movie he can't save his kids until he rediscovers his inner child and specifically how to have fun. Sounds a bit like what I went through myself and as we found out earlier according to biochemistry, it's likely that he couldn't have fun because he didn't know how to give himself permission to.

DIFFICULT IS FUN, EASY IS BORING

When I was in high school I took all the advanced placement (AP) classes. You know the ones where the classes are supposedly more difficult than regular high school classes so you can get college credits when you pass the test at the end of the class? Yeah, those are the classes I took. Only, I never took the tests at the end.

Every class would end with the same conversation:

Teacher: "You're not taking the test?"

Me: "Nope."

Teacher: "Then why did you take the class if you weren't going to take the test?"

Me: "The other classes are too easy and I get bored."

They always walked away shaking their heads, but I wouldn't have done as well in the easier classes. The boring classes couldn't hold my interest and I would underperform in them, ironically enough. Championship caliber teams sometimes do this as well and lose to the worst teams in their leagues. The announcers will talk about the teams playing down to their level instead of playing the way they normally do.

Think about something that is really boring for you. Are you interested in getting it done well? Nope. More than likely you're just interested in getting it done.

When I am challenged I always want to step up to that challenge. A perfect example of this was the Ice Bucket Challenge that went viral circa 2014. For those of you who were either not around, or not on social media, the ALS Ice Bucket Challenge was a challenge where you either donate to ALS or dump a bucket of ice water on your head. Most people ended up doing both. Then they would post the results and challenge 3 other people to do the same thing. It went like wildfire, raising about $100 Million in 1 month and received global recognition, including by many celebrities from movie stars to former presidents.

When someone challenges you to do something that you wouldn't normally do there is something inside that makes you want to prove that you can do it. Either you're proving it to them, or to yourself. You want to see if you can, or show everyone else that you can.

This is common in nature as well: if you prune a tree it will grow stronger and produce better fruit. If one wolf challenges another, there will be a fight or one will back down and there will be a new alpha. It's pressure and time that changes coal into diamonds.

A common misunderstanding of having a life of fun is the classic Aesop's Fable of the "Ant and the Grasshopper:" the Ants are working hard to store up for winter and the grasshopper is playing around enjoying the weather and not preparing.

The grasshopper mocks the ants, laughing at all their effort and telling them to stop working and enjoy the present. The ants respond with recommending that the grasshopper stores up for winter just like them.

The misunderstanding is that we can't do both at the same time. There is no reason that the ants weren't happily working towards stocking up for winter. There is nothing that keeps them from enjoying the fruits of summer and preparing for enjoying the winter. I can tell you that it's not fun nor is it part of enjoying life to starve and freeze to death during the winter.

The key to all of this is that we need to prioritize fun as part of enjoyment for life. I'm all for working hard, and planning ahead, and challenging our self. Just as I'm all for not working hard, just winging it, and doing something we're good at. In the end, it's all the same process as you set yourself up for success.

HIGH PERFORMANCE AND FUN

You get higher performance by having fun. It's true; the more fun you're having at something, the better you will do at it. I know for myself while writing a blog post or if I write a song, the really good ones just flow out of me. If I really like the topic or it's fun, time will pass at lightning speed and when I finally come up for air, I will have created something great.

Let's say that you have a task to do at work. It's not your favorite thing to do but you're good at it. Is that enough to determine a great outcome? Knowing that you're good at something, even if you're bored doing it, will you put 100% effort in? Probably not. If you don't enjoy the task, you will likely only put in enough effort to make it passable. Let's reverse the interest around now, and use the same scenario where it's something you're really good at but the task is also something that you really enjoy doing. How much effort will you put into that task? It's likely that you will give it your all and the outcome will show that effort.

If we want to perform at a high level, it is imperative that we enjoy what we are doing. The best way to do this is to make it fun. If the task is mundane or tedious, create a game that can be played while doing it. I was programming a website one time, and I had the task of taking 100 blog posts and making them all uniform. At the time I was also trying to workout and stay fit so I made a game where every time I pressed the "update" button I would do 1 squat. It ended up being a pretty tough workout but I was able to do it well because of my intention to have fun. Plus I killed two birds with one stone as I also got a bit of a workout in while working!

Nothing passes time like having fun: "time flies when you're having fun" and all that. When we're engrossed in our projects, it's easy to work 10hrs and forget that we were even working. Anytime I come up with a new invention it usually goes that way: I'll go into my shop and forget to eat and sleep. Sometimes it will be several days in a row of that; and it will result in some of my best work.

If we're assigned a project at work that we don't like to do how good of a job will we do at it? I'm sure we'll make it passable because otherwise we would constantly be looking for new employment otherwise. But, if we're assigned a task that we're really interested in, it's more likely that we will go above and beyond because we receive so much fulfillment doing it.

What's the difference?

The difference isn't really the work, although we probably worked harder and put in more hours on the project that we were excited about. The difference is attitude. We were ready to dive into that project and come up with something that we were really interested in.

So, if you're assigned a project at work that you don't like to do it find a way to have fun in the process. How good of a job will you do at it if you're enjoying yourself and how quickly will you complete it? I'm sure you'll make it passable either way so you might as well enjoy yourself. Here's another suggestion, volunteer for the task that you're really interested in, it's more likely that you will go above and beyond because you receive so much fulfillment doing it.

Just as in chapter 2 when I shared about my time working as a janitor, some tasks are harder to get to a place of enjoyment than others. No matter what we do, cleaning bathrooms falls into this category. And yet, I actually learned something then about life that I applied moving forward: I needed to clean those bathrooms regardless of whether I enjoyed doing it or not. The task still needed to get done.

Did my attitude change the outcome of the task? Nope, but it did change my life. I was able to spend time everyday praying and meditating. That time flew by because I was having fun with my time and the monotony of the task just melted away. On top of all that, they were always cleaned really well. There's something about taking thinking time while performing a menial task that brings about a thorough result. In turn, I discovered that I can have fun while doing whatever task is placed before me.

The key to high performance is learning to have fun.

PRESSURE

Pressure can be either good or bad. I was just watching the 2016 Summer Olympics and the announcer talked about the pressure getting to the athlete that just failed. It was the first dive of the competition and to the untrained eye it looked like a great jump. It's the Olympics, after all! But the announcer, who was a former Olympian herself, let us know that they weren't going to be happy with their scores, and she was right.

I think we all know that if we put too much pressure on someone it can cause them to fail. It's easiest to see in sports the correlation of pressure and success or failure, but there are other areas as well. In school for example, if we put too much pressure on either a kid in grade school or an adult in college they can crack and eventually fail, despite what they've accomplished in the past.

Pressure hits us all differently, however. The way that we react to it is not across the board. Some people actually perform better under pressure. Sports psychologists say this is based on an initial response to stress. It's a subconscious reaction that takes us into either the challenge state or the threat state: fight or flight. I believe it's based in our initial reaction of fight or flight, but I also believe that there are some simple tools that we can train ourselves to use to stay in a place of accepting the challenge and performing well, even if our initial reaction wants to be flight.

Think Big. Look at the bigger picture. In the case of sports, focus on the amazing achievements that were accomplished and the fun that was had. In school, understand that one test doesn't make or break life; it's just one area that needs more learning or greater focus. In work, make sure we have our 'Why' strong enough and we'll be fine.

Think Small. Focus on doing the basics right, and the task at hand. Oftentimes seeing the entire task as being too daunting can cause us to crumble under the pressure. Just focus on that one play, or chapter, or task. We can eat an elephant one bite at a time.

Have Fun. Don't forget to have fun. If we're not having fun, we'll start getting upset and it has been proven over and over that getting upset hinders performance. It's the classic coaches speech: "We've done the work, we deserve to be here, now go do what you do and remember to have fun."

Make a Choice. We are dealing with the fight or flight mechanism so when it comes time to step up to the challenge or back down, we need to choose right now that we will step up, no matter what we may face. Sometimes the struggle will take wanting it more than the other person. If we choose ahead of time what our response will be then we're more likely to automatically choose to step up in times of challenge.

Mindset is a big part of pressure. If we're getting pressure from outside sources then we might be looking for approval. This is where that opening proverb came into play for me. It allowed me to feel free to be me.

EQUILIBRIUM

Water loves to be in harmony with the world around it. If you put boiling hot water in a glass, it won't be long before it drops down to whatever temperature is in the room. If you took that same glass and put it into the refrigerator it wouldn't be too long before it drops down to the temperature in the refrigerator. Now, if you bring it back out of the refrigerator it's not long before it's back up to room temperature. But it won't ever go back up to that initial boiling state because it wants to be in equal to the world around it.

When water boils, it's very exciting. The bubbles are pushing the water all over the place and there is a lot of energy occurring. Water doesn't want to be that way. In fact at 211ºF water looks exactly the same as it does at 50ºF. It's not until it reaches that magic 212ºF that it starts to boil.

Now mix 211ºF water with 50ºF water and it will quickly all blend to a middle point. Without making you feel like you're back in your middle school science class, I get that we know all this stuff already but I wanted to really give you a vivid picture of what equilibrium is.

The same is true for human interaction. We will either be

the one that brings the colder water up in temperature, or we will be the one that brings the hotter water down in temperature. And all of this will be affected by the environment around us.

I talked to a woman today that told me she loves my "fun attitude." She said that for a long time, she couldn't have fun and she wanted to thank me for being a good influence on those around me. I thought that was perfect timing.

How many times are you in an environment that fun is not allowed? Church is a good example because in many sects and denominations having fun during church services is not considered respectful because we aren't being pious. I'm working to shift this mindset in my own religion, but we'll move on for now. A library seems like a rough place to try to have fun or a courtroom. For some of us, it's the home or office. It's easy to point at other places and environments that discourage having fun but isn't it us that's creating the environment in the first place?

If we want to empower ourselves to have fun, then we need to create an environment around us for fun. That doesn't mean we can't be serious and I'm not talking about being a clown. Let's try smiling wherever we go. When I started getting into triathlons, I always catch myself smiling in the middle of the race. I'm always joking that I should focus more, but I can't help it. I just want to enjoy the journey!

One thing that this does is keep us from getting burned out. Burnout is the quickest way to underperform and get hurt. This can be in sports, job, family, or personally within our own mind.

Once you burnout you start to lose focus and concentration. When you're not concentrating it's easy to make a small mistake. Then another mistake, then another. Soon you are not doing well at all. In some cases this can cause pain and suffering.

Let's turn this to you. Say for example you were on a good workout routine. Perhaps you've lost 20-30lbs with 10 more to go;

how focused then are you in getting all the way to your goal? If you burn out on training or eating healthier or following that diet/exercise plan then you are likely to lose everything you worked for.

It is common for people to get stuck on the last little bit that they need to complete at anything. With weight loss I have helped many people get free from their struggle but I can tell you this, the last 5-10% is always the hardest. Once the passion starts to fade an they accept the amazing transformation so far, it's easy to forget to finish just as strong as they started.

How about marriage?

Burnout in marriage leads to all kinds of problems from infidelity, to fighting, to kids that are getting into trouble. There are lots of things that can cause burnout but the number one thing is when it's no longer "fun" to be married. All of those other issues like financial stress and falling complacent stem back to no longer having fun in the experiences we're going through as a couple.

I have an amazing wife. She really is the best woman I could have ever found for me. During times of financial stress I wore her out with my bad attitude. It doesn't take long before someone starts to get unhappy in that situation. Let's face it: there is nothing fun about being around a crab.

With your job, once you get burned out, it's very difficult to do anything other than start a different job. Your boss will notice your work is slacking. You're coming in a bit late, leaving a bit early and your lunches are a bit longer. It takes you longer in the morning to get into the swing of your responsibilities, and you start to have problems with co-workers.

Burnout is what I call "room temperature water." It's

boring. Not cold, not hot, just blah water. So keep yourself as often as possible in an environment that brings you up, not down. If you are always in a state of growth, burnout will be far off.

The really cool thing is that it doesn't take much to turn these attitudes around. When I had my 'Aha!' moment it was a simple mindset change that started me down the path of enjoying life. All I needed was a mental and emotional reboot to get me pointed in the right direction.

My wife and I went through a reboot with our marriage not that long ago. We learned a long time ago that no matter what the problem is in marriage, if we keep in mind that the other person doesn't have ill will towards the other, it comes down to miscommunication. We fell in love for a reason, so the rest is just communication.

I must admit, I sometimes struggle to remember the reason until after we've hashed everything out and decide to let go of the issues and focus on moving forward together. For me, I decided that I would find something amazing about my wife everyday if possible and find some way to make her day better. Sometimes, I'll share my discovery with her, even something simple like seeing her beauty again, or how she smiles, or the way she is with me and the kids and telling her. Other times I will act on what I see that she "needs" and take care of something. Active listening is yet one more way I find my love for her. The result is that we are more in love than we have ever been.

The second part of equilibrium is the temperature of the water. Are we going to be the cold water or the hot water? If we're currently the cold water, theoretically speaking, then we need to be around people who are hot water. Most positive and happy people don't mind having 1 or 2 people around them that need some pick me up, it actually gives them an opportunity to spread the warmth, but if we're in a group where ½ are cold and ½ are hot then we will end up lukewarm in the middle without any form of clarity.

In all of this I'm talking about mindset, personality, how we carry ourselves, how we interact with other people, self-esteem, and how we prioritize our life. All of these areas can impact our enjoyment of life, but it starts with mindset. The rest are developed areas. The more we do good things for ourselves, and treat our self with respect, the higher our self-esteem will go.

When we're in a situation where we don't feel like having a bubbly personality or even have any desire to be around other people, it's a choice that we will make to prioritize our equilibrium and put some effort into acting in a way that we don't feel like. The goal for all of us is to create a life that we like.

WINNING ISN'T EVERYTHING, BUT LOSING STINKS

I don't talk about high performance, success, and excellence because it's fun and easy to achieve. I talk about it because life is better when we're engaged with our own lives. When we start to disconnect from one or more areas of our life, then we will start to see a negative impact. The great news is that the opposite is also true: the more we connect with every area of our life, the more we will see growth and a positive impact.

I have coached 4-12 year olds at soccer now for a long time. I actually love working with the younger ages like 5-7. When they are this little, they don't even really remember scoring or not scoring, and they also don't remember wins and losses. We don't even keep score. The kids though do know in the moment if they scored or not just not the next week.

If we were keeping score, my record as a head coach of

multiple teams is something like 90% wins. Granted, the majority of my coaching has been done with kids under 8 years old so we're not talking about World Cup Soccer here. It isn't often though that the opposing team can even score on us let alone score more goals than we do. My coaching philosophy has nothing to do with "winning" and it has nothing to do with being the best on the field. I have 1 goal in mind. Let's do the best that we can and have fun doing it.

The difference I can see is that I'm not willing to let my kids best today be their best tomorrow. I'm not ok with someone kicking the ball the wrong direction, or sitting on the field playing with grass while the game is going on. That is *not* "doing your best."

The best that these kids are capable of is far beyond the skills that they bring to the first day of practice. By the first game of each season my teams aren't kicking the ball out of bounds, and with rare occasion they aren't running the wrong direction.

I'm not focused on scoring, I'm focused on playing well and upskilling to the place of the best they can accomplish at their age in the amount of time I have to work with them. The result is that I can take any team and help them play well enough to get almost everyone on the team a goal. The ultimate outcome that I'm looking for is that the kids fall in love with playing soccer.

One season I had a girl that was very shy and timid in the beginning of the season, and by the end of the season was scoring a bunch of goals. Both her parents were high level college soccer players so they "pushed" her into soccer. After the season she came up to me with her dad, who was so proud of her. She was 5 years old and said this, "Coach, thank you for teaching me soccer. I really had fun and I like playing soccer. I just wanted to let you know that next year I won't be playing." I asked her, "Why not?" She said, "I want to dance!"

I couldn't help but smile and be so pleased with that answer.

Being great at something is fun and exciting but ultimately we have to follow our passions.

THE POWER

There is power in permission, so I give you permission to enjoy your life. We all get the same 24hrs in everyday and we all live on the same earth. If we don't like our situation we need to either change it or change you but we can't keep going forward on a downward spiral.

Use the fun philosophy as an excuse to enjoy your life. If you're a Christian like me, God has given you permission to enjoy the gift of life that He gave you. If you believe something else, then you still have permission to enjoy your life in the way that you feel makes you complete. It's your life and who can tell you that you can't enjoy it?

We all have one shot at life, how do you want it to go?

Chapter 6
TRANSFORMING FUN

---

transform - v. make a thorough or dramatic change in the form, appearance, or character

---

All of life and it's comings and goings are miraculous. If everything is mundane, "normal" and doesn't inspire any awe or wonder then this place sucks. It's no wonder that many people find it difficult to enjoy life and have fun. It's no wonder that often we live from a place of fear and powerlessness. It's easy to forget that we are miracles ourselves and that life around us is full of awe and wonder.

> There are two ways to live: you can live as if nothing is a miracle; you can live as if everything is a miracle.
>
> -Albert Einstein

When I read this quote my soul gets excited. Albert is talking more about mindset than anything spiritual. Think about what it takes for a seed to grow into a plant, create more seeds and propagate. It's a sheer miracle that must be present to multiply life and it's existence. Even dirt is full of amazing wonders! What about the inspiration of a bird in flight, or simpler, the crashing of a wave? I believe it was Einstein's childlike wonder of the everyday miraculous that allowed him to develop some of the most influential theories of our time.

I remember living from this place of the mundane...me... Mr. Happy...living from the perspective that life was everything I feared it might be! In fact, when I was battling depression I had lost my sense of awe and wonder during the time I should have embraced it the most. I can remember driving over the Pali Highway on Oahu and being irritated by the traffic and stupid drivers. The crazy thing is, this is one of the most beautiful roads I've ever driven on.

Imagine winding through a lush tropical jungle with the sun peaking through some soft clouds. There is a light rain but because it's 76ºF out and the sun is warm, the rain is a gift. As you work your way over the crest of the hill the sky opens up into a panoramic ocean view with blue lagoons and sheer lush cliffs diving down to the valley below; and a rainbow shines over the whole thing. That is pretty much every day on the Pali Highway. Yes there is traffic because it's a major thoroughfare but c'mon! How could you ignore the beauty, yet I was more concerned with the daily grind.

Whether I enjoyed my drive or was irritated by it had no bearing on the time it took to travel it. Driving that road takes 15-20 min during traffic time, regardless if I'm smiling or angry. When faced with daily struggles and challenges it can be difficult to see the beauty, or miraculous that Albert Einstein spoke about. The transformation comes from recognizing the amazing gift of life, and the beauty that surrounds us. The choice is our own in how we see life.

Here are just a few statements I hear while talking with people:

I need more joy in my life.

I can't have fun.

I was raised to believe that fun is irresponsible.

I wasn't allowed to have fun.

I don't have time for fun.

I have to work too hard.

You don't understand, I am… (insert finishing statement)

Most of the people I spoke with were very interested in this topic of fun, however, deep down they didn't believe it would be for them. The more I talk to people about this topic, the more I realize that most of us don't fully understand the transforming power of fun. It's not just about having a good time.

There is something amazing that happens when we decide to enjoy our life: for me it was life changing. Below are the abridged versions of how my life was impacted. Honestly I could write story after story of goodness, greatness, and the impossible that I have encountered on my life's journey.

MY TRANSFORMATIONS

Internal

I used to feel shame when I binged on junk food, or yelled at my kids, or took my wife for granted. I was afraid of being a failure, and letting people see who I "really" was. I was anxious about bills and how I was going to make ends meet. And I was full of stress about all of this to the point that I was crippled by back pain. It's crazy to think about, but once I started to allow myself to enjoy life; *shame, fear, anxiety,* and *stress* melted away.

I list *shame* first because I believe it's one of the single most destructive forces in our lives; and when it started to go away for me I was free to deal with the other stuff. *Fear* is close to an equal for shame, it paralyzes and tears down your spirit. *Anxiety* is the foolish cousin of fear, actually feeling the emotional pain of something before it ever even occurs. Lastly, *stress* we talked about at length in previous chapters, how it causes a lack of sleep, weight gain, and reduced libido just to name a few.

It's difficult for me to express how different I felt internally once I adopted the fun paradigm but I can tell you this; imagine all those things are no longer a part of your life and then tell me how you would feel. For me it is like I was drowning and someone threw me a bowling ball. Versus, I'm drowning and a yacht swings by and picks me up with their Jet ski. Yeah, that's the difference.

I'm trying to show the magic of it, but I don't want to mystify it. I know for myself when I was stuck, it was difficult to receive these kinds of words. At the same time, I want to paint the picture of how I feel inside right now.

I really do wake up everyday thinking about the amazing things I'm going to experience today. Just writing that down makes me cry for joy. The truth of being fully connected to life is so emotionally moving. For the first time in my life, I feel like I'm free to be me and all I want to do is help other people get to this place.

It's not all roses and sunshine, but when things do go wrong I don't dive into a spiral of shame, fear, and doubt. A good example of this is watching my kids play soccer. They are really good, I mean really good; all of them.

It's not all roses and sunshine, but when things do go wrong I don't dive into a spiral of shame, fear, and doubt. A good example of this is watching my kids play soccer. They are really good, I mean really good; all of them.

My oldest is on a competitive team playing 1 year of age above his level. My daughter is the smallest one on the field because she is 7 years old and playing with 10 year olds but she is still the best player out there. And my middle son I have to stop from scoring any more goals during his games because the league doesn't want teams to score so many points that it hurts the other kids' feelings.

Even with this talent and being on good teams, sometimes they still lose. When they do, they go home and enjoy the rest of their day. They will ask for treats for scoring goals, and tell stories of how well they played, or the funny thing one of their teammates did or said.

Kids naturally have this fun paradigm built in. My wife and I have taught our kids to always compete to win but when we do lose it's important that we grow and enjoy the process. And they get it.

Weight & Health

I've lost and gained back lots of weight over the years. I was always in better shape than my weight suggested but when you're 70+ lbs over a normal weight it's a major struggle to lose it. This final time, when I shifted my focus onto having fun and enjoying life, the diet I put myself on was easy and honestly didn't seem like anything more than just choosing a different path to walk.

In the story of my cinnamon bun catastrophe, and my wife's beautiful response, I still had to overcome the sweet tooth and get my biochemistry back in balance with good food. I started a juicing program where I juiced breakfast and lunch then ate dinner for 1 week. After that, I juiced breakfast every morning and would eat a healthy light lunch and normal dinner.

The reason it was so great for me is because I wasn't working on or focusing on the weight. As a matter of fact, that's the equivalent of focusing on the problem to get a solution. My goal was to break free from the hold that food and treats had over me.

The weight was a byproduct of my discovery.

I wrote another book on that process so I'll skip ahead a little here, but the nuts and the bolts of it were that I was having fun getting healthy and in shape. I started to enjoy the majesty of running at sunrise, and looked forward to the great feeling I had in my body from not dumping junk food into it.

I can honestly say that I went on the "Fun Diet" and lost 50 lbs and was set free from the shame and struggle of the diet yo-yo forever.

Marriage

This was probably the most dramatic transformation for me because it impacted my wife and my 4 kids. When you first get married, everything is beautiful and wonderful and exciting. Then the bills come due and we become a typical married couple as the honeymoon phase wears off.

I'm not saying we didn't have a good marriage before. My wife and I almost never fought and she always supported my craziness. She's an amazing mother, and an even better wife but when all I could see is the stress of life during the really hard times, it's like having a blinder to the gift that I had.

I'm fairly certain that my family was amazed at what an amazing wife I ended up with. Not that they believed anything different would happen, but she is seriously that wonderful.

Having said that, we hit some rough patches on several different occasions. I wrote about it in a previous chapter, but, we had some rough years of struggling financially and emotionally. There were many times that I know she was secretly crying about me and the struggle and challenge of being married.

Fifteen years later, I can honestly say that I'm more in love and happy to be married than I've ever been before: My wife and I dream together and tackle our problems together. We face any financial stress together (which is minimal these days as you'll read later). I feel like we're no longer afraid of the "WHAT IF?" question. We know that no matter the "IF" we're still committed to having fun being married. We're still committed to purposefully doing little things for each other, and making the other one smile.

When I told her what I wanted to do, she was beyond supportive. For instance, I gave up all my income to write this book, and I basically closed my business down while pretty much being the sole breadwinner. Now imagine you're in her shoes: how would you feel?!

I made sure to let her know that I'm not sure how or if I'll make any money as an author, speaker, or trainer. All she knew was that this path matters to me. Because we talk about this kind of stuff all the time, she knows my dreams and visions. She trusts that it will either work out or it won't but life is better when we try. **Wow. Quite the catch, right?!**

Parenting: Becoming Fun Dad

Falling in love with parenting and being a dad was the gift that echoes into future generations. I know my kids are better off now than they were before. Angry dad is mostly gone, and fun dad is mostly here. Even if I get upset it's not going to cause any major issues. The kids know that fun dad is right around the corner.

I feel a duty to explain what I mean by Fun Dad: I'm playful with them, and don't take the crap they put us through so seriously. If you're a parent you know what I'm talking about. I told you already about my youngest peeing on my books, and I'm sure it's the same thing in every household. As Fun Dad my role is to help direct them. Sometimes, they need a quick attitude adjustment, but for the most part if I can be the example of how they should act then they will mimic it.

I know that they mimic my bad behaviors as well, so it's no surprise that they also mimic my good behaviors. I'm actually open to hear when I'm doing something wrong because my priority isn't about being right, it's about enjoying being a dad. When I talk about being Fun Dad, I want you to know that I still discipline, and I still put them to bed at bedtime. My goal though is for them to enjoy being my kids as much as I enjoy being their dad.

My wife is much happier with my new found joy of parenting as well. When one of the kids has a bad day at school, it's a lot easier for me to come up with a good idea on how to help them deal with their emotion. Is there not a better place for them to express their feelings than at home? Most of the time kids get all bent out of shape by simple little things, and home is safe to express that. For my daughter I started gushing love on her and that seems to get her in a good space to talk about it. My boys generally need more space and my oldest usually needs some time to sort it out without my help. When I try to talk to him too soon it just takes him longer to get to the right answer. I wouldn't know that about any of my children if I didn't engage in their cares and concerns in the first place, which is the side of Fun Dad that I take very seriously.

As my kids get older and the challenges are more impactful towards the people they will become as contributing members to society, we will have a new set of challenges. I know that keeping the priority for having fun through all the stages and seasons will lead me to the right decisions for each child. It's the little things like showing our kids how to deal with stress with a smile that will help them be adjusted, happy, productive adults.

Business

One day, I looked around my desk and noticed that it was all clean. My business was doing well, and I had time to finish the projects in front of me. I was in a really good rhythm and it was fun. Until I started to have fun with my life, I had a pattern where I could only stand working at a job or business for 18 months before I had to quit and try something else. Since implementing fun into my life's journey, I have done my current business for over 5 years now and I still love doing it.

It isn't that I have finally found the one thing that I'm good at, it's that I realized I wasn't happy with my life as a whole. Before I made this realization, making a change in my approach to life every so often was exciting enough to carry me through another year and a half of living, and I thought completely switching careers was the answer. Once I "mastered" this , then I wanted to move on. People used to call me the Jack of All Trades, Master of None. I despised that moniker, but how could I deny it? Just look at all the different things that I was a part of: Internet Technician, Mechanic, Retail Clothing, Customer Service, Sales, Radio DJ and Promotions Director, Pastor, Magazine Publisher, Motivational Speaker, Graphic Designer, Automobile Transport Broker, Real Estate Agent, Television Advertising Exec, Website Developer, and a whole host of odd jobs here and there.

Now, being a Jack-of-All-Trades is a badge of honor. I've learned how to focus my mind and ambitions. And when it all comes down to it, what really happened is that I learned how to enjoy my life, and it leaked into my business. I'm not naturally a details kind of guy so you can imagine that I would get tired of programming websites fairly quickly. I had found a way to enjoy what I was doing and stopped looking for something that I might like doing.

Most of us are smart enough to be able to be good enough at a job in about a year's worth of time to start getting bored of the daily grind. The key for me was learning how to enjoy my life as a whole and have fun. Once I did that, then it leaked into my business and everything started to click. I was free to have fun doing something that I would have otherwise ran from because it became boring.

For example, in the past I don't think I could have written a book. Even though I've always liked to write, the idea of writing thousands of words everyday then editing, proofing and tweaking is a very daunting task. Honestly, in the past I probably would have been bored with my subject before I even got finished writing about it. I found that I thoroughly enjoy the process of writing, researching and rewriting; even the editing is fun. It's amazing how finding passion for life seems to spill over into areas that are otherwise not fun.

Business started to come easy for me, and my ideas about finances changed. It's this mindset shift that really allowed my wife and I to get free from financial struggle. We were more open to following the path of success. It's funny because saying it like that seems quite basic but looking back, I can honestly say that we were either afraid of success or afraid of failure. Or both!

I'll never forget some of the greatest advice I received from my father-in-law: Prior to my epiphany we were out shopping and I got into a conversation with someone that we saw about my work and I was very honest with them about how I felt about it. After we left that store, he took me aside and quite passionately said that "whenever someone asks you how your business is, tell them it's great. Tell them it's the best thing that ever happened to you. Tell them all the great stuff that it's bringing to your life. When you're done, they should want to change careers to do what you're doing."

I was shocked at first, thinking that it wasn't an honest

approach, but as I really looked at the meaning of the words behind what he was saying, I really took it to heart. I started to implement it, but I didn't get to realize the full power of what he was saying until I started to prioritize fun in my life. It's not about being fake, or lying or not being "real." It's just being honest about all the great stuff that you're doing. People don't really want to hear that I am struggling just like them; they want to hear about my passions and the things that make me come alive. It goes back to an equilibrium thing: do I want to come down to their level or do I want to pull them up to mine?

Once I started being optimistically honest about the amazing things that I was able to do, like working from home or making my own hours, etc...I began to find that I was really freeing myself up to fully enjoy what I do. Focusing on all the good things while dealing with the challenges is constantly reinforcing my "WHY."

NEAR DEATH EXPERIENCES

Some get "forced" into this optimistic approach for life after almost dying or having what we commonly know as near death experiences. If you've ever met someone who has come face to face with their own mortality, you will likely talk to someone who has a "new lease on life."

I've met a few people like this in my time. I have a friend from Cambodia who is the greeter at his church. He is one of the most joy filled people you will ever meet, and he was dead ... I mean, DEAD. He had drowned in the river while fishing. The details are a little tough in the translation but it seems as though it was a boating accident. They fished him out of the river, and his family had started preparations for the funeral. They built a casket for him and had prayer and mourning time over the next couple of days. During one of their prayer sessions, right before they were going to bury him, he came back to life.

They had all been praying for this to occur, but they never really thought it would happen. The whole room was stunned! He sat up and decided to go for a walk. The whole village knew he had died so when he was walking around they freaked out and yelled, "Ghost! Ghost! Ghost!"

He got scared that there was a ghost somewhere in the village and it was following him, so he ran home and told his family to stay inside because there is a ghost outside. They then told him that he was the ghost, and then began his transformation.

Whether it was a miracle and God sent him back or he was in a coma for 2-3 days is really irrelevant for the story. He knows better than all of us that life is short, and you only get a certain amount of time here on earth. Are you going to waste it being miserable or are you going to enjoy it every second that you can?

I have another friend who almost died in a cycling accident during a race. Ronnie Toth was involved in a crash, and got launched into a barrier. He hit the corner of it going really fast and broke most of the bones in his face. After multiple surgeries from multiple surgeons fixing him up, he has healed and got back on the bike. Now he is one of the most joyful people to be around.

Here is Toth's Story:

> My background is as a runner turned Ironman Triathlete turned cyclist. I've raced everything from the 24 hour solo mountain bike world championships, to category 1 pro road races, over 100 triathlons, as well as cyclocross, and now Red Hook fixed gear races.

In 2014 I had a horrible accident during the Manhattan Beach Grand Prix where I was bumped into a gate at 80kph and broke every bone in my face and my bicep bone came through the skin. I was in a coma for a week and in the hospital for 3 weeks.

In this life hard times are going to beat us up. I nearly lost my life in that bad crash. Shortly after, the closest person in my life disappeared. I could have felt sorry for myself and become depressed, but instead I crawled to the mirror after getting out of the coma and I said to myself "the person that you become through this is who you will be for the rest of your life."

Who we are in the darkest times in life is who we become when the light shines. We have not been given a spirit of fear, but of power, and of love, and of clear mind. We must choose to thrive through adversity. You can quit but you will eventually have to stand up, not quit and begin moving again. If you get knocked down 8 times you must learn to stand again each time. Thrive On

"It takes surprisingly very little to be happy, I think we got lost somewhere along the way in chasing security or the illusion therein. Life is a vapor. You could be here today and gone tomorrow. Enjoy your life. 70 years plus or minus, how will you use them?"

— Toth

What a story! He truly is an amazing human being. Surprisingly, it's normal for people to have life changing transformations when they have something traumatic happen to them. Often times with near death experiences people realize that life is too short and they do all the things that they've always wanted to do but never did instead of making a list of them and never acting on them.

How do we get that same transformation for ourselves without almost being eaten by a shark or coming out of a 6 month coma? It's simple: Do fun stuff!

If you want to learn how to surf, go on vacation somewhere that you can surf. If you've always wanted to play the guitar, go for it! Walk into a music shop and see about if they have guitars to rent if you don't want to invest in purchasing one until you've learned how to play. Five minutes per day is all it takes to become a guitar player in 2 months. If you want to see Paris, book your trip right now! If finances are holding you back, you can still put together your itinerary, sign up for flight deals, and you may be surprised how affordable it really is to act on your dreams.

It doesn't have to be an epic trip or purchase that requires lavish expenses; you can keep it simple. Go to the park every day for lunch to get out into nature more. Make time to read that book you've had for months and can't get to. Start running every day or sign up for a meetup group that is doing something you're interested in. Whatever you do, start doing fun stuff.

If you don't make life a priority, then it will continue on without you. For me, every area of my life is impacted simply because I choose fun. Start choosing fun whenever you have the opportunity.

Think about the things you do in the areas that you might not be enjoying, or are stuck. Are they productive or destructive? Are you having a good attitude or are you grumpy and bored? Do your dreams and desires feel insurmountable? Ask yourself good questions about what you're feeling, doing, and choosing. Be honest, not mean. We are really good at being hard on ourselves.

I want you to be honest but not harsh and self-deprecating. Find out what's really going on inside, and then get help if you need it. You'll discover so much more about yourself if you're willing to inwardly reflect after asking "What do I want?" and then list out the answers.

The quality of the answer completely depends on the quality of the question. It usually takes many questions to get you to the right one. I remember talking to my wife about being nervous with a somewhat risky investment. In talking with her I said, "Will you still love me if I lose all of our money?"

She said, "I loved you before we had money, so yes, I will still love you if we lose it all."

I knew that was true, but it didn't alleviate the fear I was having as the provider of our family. Then the right question came to me: "If I lose everything will I still love me?"

I started bawling my eyes out and it was easy to get to the place where we were both good with taking the risk. I took the risk and it worked out in our favor but I didn't get out in time and eventually we did end up with a small loss. Yet I didn't care and she didn't care. It was a good experience and lesson learned as I was able to cross an internal bridge and grow.

"It's not the reality that shapes us but the lens from which you view the world that shapes your reality. And if we can change the lens, not only can we change your happiness we can change every educational and business outcome at the same time."

- Shawn Achor

HOW DOES HAVING FUN TRANSFORM

There is some amazing research in the field of psychology about the impact of how focusing on the right things positively impacts every area of our life. The most popular course in the history of Harvard University is Positive Psychology 1504 by Tal Ben-Shahar (PhD). The course is 22 lectures, roughly 75 minutes each, about the psychological aspects of life fulfillment and flourishing, which teaches empathy, friendship, love, achievement, creativity, spirituality, happiness, and humor.

Only 10% of your outside world impacts your overall happiness. They are finding out that 90% of your long term happiness is determined by how your brain processes the world.

The majority of the world works like this: if I work harder then I will have more success, if I have more success then I'll be happier. This is how we parent, manage, work, & create motivation. And yet, this approach is totally backwards from how the brain functions. What we're doing is creating an impossible goal for ourselves: If we hit our sales target, then we raise the goal. And what's extremely detrimental to society is that we were conditioned to believe this way since grade school. If we get good grades, then we need to get better grades, and if we behave well at home then we get the reward.

The problem with this is that we lose out on the "Happiness Advantage." according to Shawn Achor and his book *The Happiness Advantage*. Think of this like having the element of surprise; once you've given up the element of surprise then you lose that advantage. When you are operating from a place of happiness, joy, calm, etc. then you are more likely to be successful.

Shawn Ahcor's group found that your brain when in a positive state is 31% more productive than when it's in a negative state. You're 37% better at sales, doctors are 19% more accurate at coming up with the solution than when neutral, negative, or stressed.

Below are daily steps to start building your happiness up over the next 28 days. You only need to do them for a few minutes at a time, so I'm not asking you to train for a marathon or write an epic novel. Do them all back to back or spread throughout the day.

DAILY STEPS TOWARDS HAPPINESS:

Be Thankful: Write more than one thing that you are grateful for. I recommend doing it on social media to spread the joy. Use **#FUNdamentalBook** They can be big things like your spouse, children, house, job, etc. Or, they can be small things like living in an area with lots of trees or the joy of a good avocado.

Keep Notes: Write 1 positive thing that you have experienced over the last 24hrs. This is different than being grateful, but can still be related. You can keep this one private if you want, but remember there is tremendous value in relating stories to your social circles. Use **#FUNdamentalBook**

Get Moving: Get up and move intentionally. You can keep it brief if you have to. Park at the back of the parking lot, take the stairs, or complete a full workout. Do what you can but get up and move for 21 days in a row. I have a cool exercise plan that can be done anywhere at any skill level. If you want to download it go to my website: *www.ryan8.com/TheFunDiet*

Pray or Meditate: Simply calm down and focus on your breathing.

Anyone can meditate for 2 minutes. For those of you who pray (like me), this is more of a time to just listen to what God is saying. Do not try to have a conversation or talk about your needs. Instead just listen to what God is saying.

Intentional Acts of Kindness: Do one intentionally kind thing. It can be as simple as starting your day with 1 positive message to someone praising them. Or it could be a gift for your loved ones, which I like to do from time to time. It could even be buying a drink for a stranger in line at the coffee shop.

One of the greatest ways to experience a transformation in your own life is start small and read things that are inspirational. Here are a few quotes to get you going:

"There is only one success - to spend your life in your own way."

- Christopher Morley, American journalist, novelist, and poet.

"I am still determined to be cheerful and happy, in whatever situation I may be; for I have also learned from experience that the greater part of our happiness or misery depends upon our dispositions, and not upon our circumstances."

- Martha Washington, The first First Lady of the United States

"Be happy while you're living, for you're a long time dead."

- Scottish Proverb

"Whoever is happy will make others happy too. He who has courage and faith will never perish in misery."

- Anne Frank, holocaust survivor

"I'm so optimistic, I'd go after Moby Dick in a row boat and take the tartar sauce with me."

- Zig Ziglar, American author and motivational speaker

"Happiness lies in the joy of achievement and the thrill of creative effort."

- Franklin Roosevelt, 32nd president of the United States

"The secret of happiness is not in doing what one likes, but in liking what one does."

- James M. Barrie, Author of Peter Pan

"Don't limit investing to the financial world. Invest something of yourself, and you will be richly rewarded."

- Charles Schwab, American Businessman

Most of us would be upset If we were accused of being "silly." It comes from the old English word "seilig" and it's literal definition is to be blessed, happy, healthy and prosperous."

- Zig Ziglar, American author and motivational speaker

Chapter 7
HEALING FUN

healing - v. the process of making or becoming sound or healthy again

HEALING FUN

Life is hard. It's wrought with challenges ranging from physical labor to emotional strain to natural disasters. There are many things that can suck the life from us and make the idea of having fun almost impossible to grab a hold of. Even the thought of having a normal life can seem out of reach. Healing is what we need to repair the damage and begin to live again.

Cancer, the big "C" word these days, has ravaged everyone we know. Most of us have a relative who has had or is currently dealing with cancer. Children are getting rare and crazy diseases and other life threatening issues that have never been seen or heard of before. Suicide is the #2 killer of people between the ages of 15-29 and the average person around the world is on some kind of medication for physical or mental issues.

It's obvious that things aren't getting any better. Whenever we fix one area then something else pops up. The world is sick and in the spirit of "misery loves company" we globally want others to be sick as well.

The amount of chronic pain that exists is staggering. If you ask a room of 100 people if anyone is in pain most of the room will raise their hands. The most common pain in the world today is Lower Back Pain while second to that is Neck Pain or Migraines. The frequency of this is beyond ridiculous. It is more common for people to have chronic pain then to be pain free.

I suffered from low back pain for the better part of 20 years but it was for a good 15 of those years that I was typically crippled by it every other month for a week. I don't have back pain anymore, which I'll go into more detail on shortly.

If the whole world is sick or in pain, it makes sense to me that there is a systemic problem that needs to be addressed. Here's what I have noticed:

In the 80's it was popular to have ulcers, so everyone struggled with ulcers. In the 90's people had migraines, the #1 chronic pain at the time. Now we have transitioned into back pain, and probably soon we will transition into something else, possibly major food allergies.

Right now gluten intolerance and Crohn's disease are on a huge upturn. I remember when everyone was allergic to lactose and before that it was MSG. There are actually studies that prove the MSG allergy is mostly bogus. The Food Network did a study where they cooked food for 50 participants. Half of them had known MSG allergies, and the other half were either tolerant or didn't know one way or the other.

They served foods where they told everyone that half of plates have MSG in them and they will be serving them at random. Then they wanted the participants to let them know if they are having a reaction. The majority of the MSG sufferers raised their hands and described what was happening to them.

Then the big reveal: None of the food contained MSG.

So what happened? They quizzed some of the ones who had raised their hands and asked them what they think was going on. One lady said she must have had something earlier with MSG in it, but c'mon! Talk about reaching for something.

They did a wrap up at the end of the show with a bunch of research that basically proved that the vast majority of MSG sufferers (not everyone obviously) didn't actually have a problem with MSG.

LOWER BACK PAIN

I'm going to give you my secret as to how I healed my lower back pain. It all started when I was in a sales meeting with someone and I had hobbled to our meeting place early so I could be the first to sit down but I was obviously in pain. This was day 3 of my normal 7 day process of going from collapsing on the floor after bending over to pick up something as simple as a sock to laying on the couch for 5 days straight.

I had tried everything. Chiropractors couldn't help until the muscles relaxed which was after day 5 and they did a good job of getting me back into alignment. But it didn't matter, I would go back out again. I was told I probably needed surgery, bulging discs and arthritis and all that crap.

The person I was meeting with told me about a book called *Healing Back Pain* by Dr. Sarno and it helped her husband overcome his back pain without surgery. That was good enough for me! I bought the book and started reading. Crazy enough, the answer was simple. The book didn't have any tips or tricks or how to's in it at all. It was more of a biographical look at how this doctor used a simple notion to get people healed from back pain for over 25 years.

The main concept was this: emotional pain is far worse than physical pain. When you are faced with an emotional struggle, your body will defend itself by causing a physical pain to distract you from it. For me this was stress and fear associated with taking care of my family financially. The solution was to have an internal conversation about what's going on whenever the chronic pain would arise.

Well, it worked. Every time my back started to go out on me, I would work on my internal struggles. I talked with my wife about what was going on, and I had many self conversations. It took about 2-3 years to get past it altogether, but the problems became less frequent the whole time. The key was very simple, the pain starts, I check in with myself emotionally, talk it out with someone I trust, then the pain starts to go away. Today I haven't had a problem in several years.

SO WHAT'S MY POINT?

There is a correlation between what's going on inside someone's soul that affects their physical body. The soul for my purposes consist of the *Mind, Will* & *Emotions*. I have used this exact point to help people lose weight and overcome addiction.

I've already shown how our bodies are affected biochemically by various emotions. If you're stressed, it activates your fight or flight mechanism and does crazy stuff with your hormones. If you're elated, your body releases a host of chemicals to help you enjoy it. Science is behind the notion that how we feel emotionally impacts our physical being.

The **Mind** represents our knowledge and understanding. It is the central computer for how we internally process all things external. It is responsible for creating the lens by which we see the world.

Our **Will** is the conscious and unconscious part of our

psyche. It is responsible for our deliberate actions. While the *Mind* holds the lens for our psyche, the *Will* holds the mechanisms for how we act and react.

Emotions are the "feelings" part of us. When we feel sadness, joy, remorse, peace, calm, stress, etc., those all belong to our emotional being.

When our feelings or *Emotions*, are hurt either by an expectation that wasn't met or from loss, then we create an action, *Will*, for how to deal with the pain. We use our lens, *Mind*, as the basis for the decision. If our family dog dies, we would likely be sad. How we deal with that sadness will be different for everyone. That's why they say people deal with grief in many different ways.

There are other things that cause grief. Our children cause us grief frequently. I told the story of the pee pee books earlier where my son peed all over my books; this caused me grief. Getting phone calls from a bill collector 17 times a day caused me tons of grief. If the grocery store is out of my favorite whatever that can cause grief.

It's no wonder then that our actions and attitudes on a daily basis are somewhat predictable. I believe this is one of the reasons divorce is so high these days. If you act a certain way for years in a row, why would anything you say or do for a short period of time prove anything about the future. Once you are put under the same circumstances you are likely to behave the same way again. Right?!

> **The only way to truly get to a place of change is to heal your soul.**

Healing your soul starts with changing the lens. How you see the world is the basis for all actions and judgments. The field of Positive

Psychology states that only 10% of your exterior world impacts your long term happiness. It's the internal stuff, soul, that is responsible for long term happiness.

Tal Ben-Shahar is a Harvard professor who teaches the most popular class in the history of Harvard, Positive Psychology. The main thought is: If something terrible can scar someone for life as in Post Traumatic Stress then so too could something fantastic and wonderful uplift one's life forever.

Positive Psychology is somewhat of a new area of study in the field of Psychology but to be perfectly honest, this isn't a "new" concept. Most of the greatest coaches in sports already did this instinctually. Some may know it as morale, but the idea is that it's far better to focus on the good things than the bad things. It's better for people to think about the potential positive outcome than the negative.

As we go through life we create markers through specific events that happen to us. These markers can be triggers for behavior. If someone calls us something hurtful over and over and treats us in a certain way, whenever we hear that word, we will feel the same pain even if it's not being directed at us. This has been associated with addiction and other self-defeating attitudes and actions, which tears us down, but it can also be used in a positive way to reprogram and heal by replacing the negative triggers with positive ones.

A good example is comfort food. The food itself is usually not very good for you, but because mom or grandma used to make it all the time when you were growing up you feel comfort from eating it as an adult. You have been programmed to feel good things from simply eating a specific food.

> Finally, brethren, whatever is true, whatever is honorable, whatever is right, whatever is pure, whatever is lovely, whatever is of good repute, if there

is any excellence and if anything worthy of praise, dwell on these things.

- Philippians 4:8

REMEMBER THE BIG WINS IN YOUR LIFE

A great exercise for creating positive markers and triggers in our life is to remember the big wins. We can start when you were a kid and your team won the championship, or even that time we got an A+ on that test or paper we wrote. If that's too far back, recall the good things in life that we can hold onto.

It may be when a child being born, or that amazing job that opened so many doors. It could be the epic vacation we went on with all of the good memories to hold onto. There are several YouTube videos floating around that talk about "Dad Wins" where dads catch their children just seconds from a rough fall or something dangerous. They are really funny yet inspiring as it helps us remember the things in life that we do well. In this case, it was dads, but there is inspiration all around us.

Find something that inspires you and then surround yourself with it. I am always impressed by the triathletes that I race with. These are some of the most amazing people on the planet. Because I like being around those people, and I enjoy doing triathlons I have made it a goal to do 2-3 per year.

LET THE HEALING BEGIN

We have all heard that laughter is the best medicine, but official research on the subject isn't extensive. However, there are actually laughter therapists, which is funny in itself. The majority of the research can't really differentiate between the actual laughing, having a positive outlook, a good sense of humor or having family and friends around being the source of healing. There is one thing that the studies do show to be true though, and that's when we're enjoying your life, we tend to be healthier and recover more quickly.

I met a man the other day who was given the cancer death sentence with 3 months to live. That was 3 years ago. I was shocked, so I asked him what he did. His response was perfect: "Nothing directly but I decided to go out and do all the things I've always wanted to accomplish before I die." His situation isn't unique, I've found that there are many who extend their lives beyond the doctor's estimates simply by living the lives they've always wanted.

I say it all the time: if you're not having fun, then what's the point? I healed my back pain by breaking free from the emotional stress and strain of holding onto the outcome of my family's happiness. It was affecting me physically, but once I was able to release my own false sense of control over my life, only then was I free to truly live.

During that same time my wife started experiencing nosebleeds all the time. We lived in Hawaii, so you know it's not dry air. It was definitely disconcerting, but ultimately those went away as well once the stress level dropped dramatically.

We eat pretty healthy: all organic and homemade, limiting our processed food and refined sugars intake. At this same time though, it seemed like our kids were sick all the time. I know this is common in large families. One kid gets sick, then another, then another, then another, then mom, then dad, then it goes around again. When people would comment about our kids being sick all the time I couldn't help but be defensive, yet if I was honest, deep down I knew they were right.

Last year my son had perfect attendance at school and my daughter only missed a few days due to illness. What brought about the difference? I made it a priority to make sure my kids were enjoying their lives. Part of that is taking the time to sit and listen to them, but honestly it's easy for kids to love their lives when mom and dad aren't arguing and yelling at them.

We now have a house committed to enjoying life, being positive and doing things that are specific for each kid to add to their overall enjoyment of life. We now make FUN a priority.

When I talk about prioritizing fun, I am talking about creating a life that we enjoy. I'm talking about waking up everyday ready for what the day has to bring us. I'm talking about making our life one that's worth living.

I'm not asking anyone to quit their jobs although sometimes that's a necessary change. I'm not asking anyone to do anything physically drastic. And I don't want a person to set up any unnecessary expectations, especially if they are unattainable, which can cause an adverse effect. Unachievable expectations can set us up for failure. It's so much more freeing to expect the unexpected.

CHANGE YOUR LENS

How to get the healing that you're after starts with changing your lens. Remember the MIND is responsible for creating your base of understanding. All your actions and reactions stem from your perspective.

I'll prove it to you.

In a dark alley a man is standing over a body, he has a bloody knife in his hand and he's trying to figure out what to do. Who is he?

The obvious answer is that he's the murderer but if I told you that he is wearing a badge and the knife is in an evidence bag it completely changes the story and the scene.

The difference is simply the base of understanding. The same is true for our lives: If you are not happy with your life, there is the possibility that you have painted yourself into a corner. More than likely in this situation, you simply need to change your perspective.

STEP 1 CHANGE YOUR PERSPECTIVE

It's not hard. If you think this world is messed up and going to hell in a handbasket then you will treat people like they have no hope and you will be defensive. If however, you believe people to be inherently good and they are doing their best to make it through a world that lies to them and beats them up, then it's a lot easier to have compassion and forgive someone for cutting you off on the freeway.

This part is going to be completely up to you, but one way or the other you have to get a positive outlook. Changing to a positive outlook can be as simple as making the decision to see things differently.

Picture a glass of water filled about half way. Now hold it in your hand and tell me, how heavy is that glass of water? I'll bet you thought I was going to ask you if it's half full or half empty.

The thing about that glass of water is that it doesn't matter what the absolute weight is. What matters is how long you are holding it for. If you hold it for a few minutes, it's light and not a burden. If you hold it for an hour, it's heavier and your hand may start cramping up. If you hold it all day long without shifting any of the weight, it becomes impossible to continue holding in the same position.

All the things that you're worried about or are dealing with are like that glass of water. How long you think about them will determine their impact on you. Think about them just a little and nothing happens, but if you think about them for a few days you're likely to be hurt. If you think about them for years you will likely have a major issue with something that started out like a small glass of water.

The decision as to how long you want them to impact your life is simply a matter of choice. The same is true about how you want to interpret the things around you. This is the key to changing your lens.

I chose to prioritize fun as a key to enjoying life. While it's not always Priority #1 or even #2, it's rarely lower than #5 and sometimes it remains #1.

STEP 2 ALIGN YOUR WILL

Just because you're not sick doesn't mean you are healthy. It's not good enough to simply have a positive outlook. The next step is to align your will with your new found perspective. Your will is your belief system in action. It takes 28 days to create a new habit. I have broken them down into weeks.

Week 1: Preparation - Don't do anything too drastic. Simply give yourself the best opportunity to enjoy the next 28 days. You are doing things that will contribute to the overall success of making a permanent change but you don't actually change anything in the first week. Do your research, and get your mind ready to make some changes. Make your lists, and get prepared.

Week 2: Reframing - This week is supposed to be fun, but you should be challenged. In Week 1 you weren't supposed to change anything, while in this week I want you to change everything as much as possible. Regardless of what habit you're trying to create or break it's important that whatever you are doing this week looks completely different from the week before. If you're trying to get a better life attitude, then correct your statements out loud when you recognize that you're having a poor attitude. If you're trying to quit smoking, then change to a different brand of cigarettes, change what hand you smoke with and even change what time you smoke. If you normally smoke after you eat, then smoke before you eat. The idea is to shake your world up.

Week 3: Creation - This week is full of journaling, self talking and any other internal tools you have found to work for you. This is the week that you create the world that you want. If you want more time in the morning to focus, then you need to get up earlier or adjust your schedule to accommodate. This is the week where you find out what works and what doesn't that you have already put into practice from Week 2: Reframing. If we continue with the example of quitting smoking from Week 2, then this is the week that you go cold turkey. What we have done in the reframing week is to create a pattern interrupt for your brain. So in the third week, it's ready to receive a new concept.

Week 4: Success - This week all the things that you did through the first 3 weeks come into full view and you get to share your success with the world. If you're trying to break a deep-seeded addiction, there is a bit more to it but for permanent healing, but for just changing your actions to match your perspective you should be good to go. Take this week seriously and be intentional about the new life that you created for yourself. Tell people about your new change, and continue to stay disciplined on doing things right.

Oftentimes, when we implement something new like a shifted behavior, we will be challenged by people who know us and are familiar with our old ways. They may even call us phony or they may think that we are being fake. It's not true. Just because we chose to accentuate negative things before doesn't mean that accentuating the positive things are a lie. They always existed, we just may have never seen them before.

When I was in high school, I made a new friend and went over to his house for the first time. His dad was one of those people who considers themselves a good judge of character. He liked me right off, but always had one eye on me.

About 2 months later, he came up to me and started asking me a few questions. Ultimately, he asked:

"Ryan, are you for real?"

"What do you mean?" I asked, not really knowing what he meant.

"I've been watching you and you seem to always be happy," he stated. "You're always polite and well mannered. You seem like a good boy and are very confident around adults."

"Um. Thanks."

He continued, "I can generally peg someone right out the gate, but you're a mystery to me. I can't tell if you're for real or if you just blowing smoke up my ass."

"I'm not really sure what you mean, but I am this way all the time."

"You really are, aren't you?"

"Yep."

You may get the same thing when people see the new change in you. Rest assured that when it's real, people will know, even if it takes them a little bit of time to realize this. Not everyone is used to authenticity in another person's behavior. It may take some time for them to get used to the new you, but trust me, there is nothing fake about behaving in a way that makes your life and those around you more enjoyable.

STEP 3 MANAGE YOUR EMOTIONS

I've said it before: emotions are liars. They are the irrational chemical reactions in your body that make you "feel" a certain way. You can be in complete danger and feel like superman, or you can be in a place of peace and bliss and feel lost and miserable.

Do not discount your emotions just because they are liars. Our feelings are real and they are valid. Once we have shifted our perspective and aligned our actions, it will be easier to recognize emotions that aren't serving us or are lying to us. Use positive reinforcement techniques of the things that are going well in your life.

There are a few emotions that are crippling and dangerous which we should eliminate from our world as soon and as often as possible. I do believe there is a place for them in a healthy balanced life, but they get way too much air play, especially when in the middle of a transition.

First is shame. Shame is what you feel when you know you've done something wrong that someone else would be disappointed by. It's appropriate to feel shame if you cheat on your wife. It's not appropriate to feel shame when you fail at something.

If you try your best and you fail, there is no shame in it. I have gone to the grocery store late at night to get diapers and returned home victorious only to learn that I came home with the wrong size: FAIL. I tried to do it right. I didn't try to do it wrong. I looked at the sizes and made a decision. But it was 12:30 at night and Walmart has some distracting people hanging around that late, so I made a mistake.

You have to be allowed to make mistakes. If you're willing to take responsibility for your mistake and move forward towards doing it right or better the next time, then there is no shame in it. People can forgive a mistake when it's met with a contrite heart and a willingness to be coached.

When I learned to play the drums I got some great advice that I have applied to every area of my life. I was trying to teach myself the drums so I didn't have expert guidance. A friend of mine was a studio to drummer and had toured with a handful of bands. He told me that he could fix my drumming problems with one sentence: If you're going to make a mistake make it as loud as you possibly can. The key to being a good drummer is to trust your internal rhythm. Sure, it takes years of practice to be great, and there's constantly new beats that require messing up quite a bit, but the only way to become great is to detach from the shame of doing it wrong.

The fear of making a mistake leads to the shame of that mistake being real. So Fear is the other emotion to avoid as much as possible.

Fear accentuates pain and prevents success. I'm not talking about being smart or cautious, although being too cautious is fear in action. I am talking about allowing fear to paralyze you. I'm talking about allowing the fear of something unknown to reach out and take you down before you ever had the chance to get it right.

My wife teaches pain-free childbirth. That's right, she has

had 4 babies completely pain free without the use of drugs and she teaches other women how to experience the same thing. One of her big points is all about removing fear.

Fear will actually multiply pain. Think about a drunk getting in a car accident, or someone sleepwalking. Because they are in a lessened state of awareness the triggers for fear and pain don't exist and the result is they get hurt a lot less than the other people involved. Children are a great example of this as well, by distracting them from their boo boo they stop crying and go back to playing much quicker. If they look at the "owie" then you start to see the tears well up and pain sets in.

Fear does the same thing to our relationships, health, business, etc… The more you allow fear to be the deciding factor, the more you will make a poor decision. If you're afraid that your friend is lying to you, then you will not allow them to be close to you, essentially blocking the relationship from growth and further connection. Many good relationships have been severed due to fear from rejection that direct communication would have overcome.

Fear of rejection will cause people to reject others. Fear of success will make people sabotage their business. Fear of failure will make people fail so they can be right. Fear has never been helpful to us in everyday life. It causes the fight or flight mechanism in us and both fighting or flighting are only good when in a legitimately dangerous situation.

HEALING IS A MUST

You really don't have a choice if you want to live a life of abundance. You must heal. You must repair the wounds of your life. You know that old saying, "Scars fade and wounds heal, but glory lives forever."

That is only true if the wounds heal.

Without redemption, there is no transformation. It's important to relay the stories of your life to others. If not in a general settings, then in private settings to people who you know will understand. Redemption does not necessarily mean that the previous pain or issue didn't take place. It's simply that who you are today doesn't have to be who you were yesterday.

Redeption is a road less traveled. You can go at it on your own but it's much easier if you have someone to share it with. It's time to take the bandages off and start allowing your wounds to heal properly. You are strong, and courageous!

Chapter 8
YOUR STORY

story - n. an account of past events in someone's life or in the evolution of something

Life is full of seasons. In the winter it's cold, in the summer it's hot, in the spring it's wet and in the fall it's windy. Life throws things at us and how we respond and react in those seasons will determine our long-term happiness. The winter is peaceful, the summer is freedom, the spring is growth and the fall is reflection.

I'm living in California, with my smoking hot amazingly powerful wife and our four wonderful children, I work for myself, we own our home, and yes, I'm truly happy. Similar situation to the beginning of the book but with a different outcome from the depressed winter that I was in. I no longer want to hide in a hole. When I'm faced with adversity, I accept the challenge and I move forward knowing that as long as I keep in mind the joy that has brought me this far will make anything that comes ok. No matter what season I'm in now, I can find the good that comes from these challenges.

What season are you in?

What are the things that are bringing you down?

What are the tools that you can use to pull yourself free?

You will go through summer and feel free and go through winter and have peace. You will go through spring and have growth, and you will go through fall and need reflection. The question is are you going to react to your life or are you going to plan your life. I say it all the time, are you creating your life or is life creating you. You will go through all four seasons, whether it's with joy or with struggle will be based on the lens you use and the choices you make.

How you live is writing your story. How you act, react, and feel, determine your life's outcome.

In the book by Paulo Coelho called *The Alchemist*, the main character is told by Melchizedek, the King of Salem, that he is writing his own "personal legend" which is a main theme of the book. I loved this idea that my legend is a growing tale of how I lived. It's the story of my life with the ups, downs, lefts, rights, and everything else in between. It really made me consider what kind of a legacy I wanted to leave for my children.

You've already written part of your personal legend. The good news is that the rest of the story is yet to be written. What do you want to accomplish and what dreams do you want to fulfill? What decisions do you need to make to get you from Point A to Point B? What journey will that create for you in the process?

I want my kids to say, "My dad was the most amazing man in the whole world." I want the people around me to think I'm the most interesting man in the world. I want my wife and I to live a storybook life together. When I'm done, I want to have a story worth telling: Full of adventure, excitement, drama, adversity, and overcoming.

The reason I want this is for my story to inspire others to greatness. I remember listening to my Dad talk about how he and his buddy biked across Europe. He could say things in many languages, and he had all these really cool trinkets he picked up along the way. I remember that moment in my life like a movie. We were at my step-mom's apartment in Vista, California and It was the evening. My sister and I gathered around the coffee table as my dad relayed stories which shaped my life forever.

One moment in time created a marker for me and how I wanted to live. I fell in love with language, and geography. It stirred adventure inside of me and I told myself at 9 years old that I wanted to be just like my dad.

Now that I'm older, I know that this was a very short time in his life's story. He's not even friends with that guy anymore. As epic of a journey as the story sounded, I'm sure it was full of challenges and difficulties. I'm sure it was dangerous at times, and cold and wet and miserable on some of the days. I'm sure they were hungry sometimes, and probably had to sleep in awful places along the way. The story that inspired me though was to pursue a life of knowledge and adventure. I wanted to do well in school so I could know as much as my Dad and go on my own epic journey.

The world doesn't need you to be good. It needs you to come alive. Whether you physically go on a journey or mentally travel, your life needs you to be full of passion and to fully connect with the power of YOU. Your story is as important as mine. What is your story going to look like? What kind of a legacy do you want to leave?

For a long time I didn't even know what my passions were. I believe that passions change all the time but if we look hard enough there is likely to be a theme for how we pursue life. If we don't like how that is going, then make the change. Sort priorities, and make space for the life we want to live.

IT'S TIME TO ASK YOURSELF, "WHAT DO I WANT THE STORY OF MY LIFE TO LOOK LIKE?"

WRITE YOUR STORY

What does this story look like?

How have you lived?

Who are the people that are in your story?

What kinds of struggles did you overcome?

What adventures did you go on?

Did you run into any trouble or was there danger?

Did you get hurt or did you get through it unscathed?

Where did you live?

Did you live in one place for the rest of you days or did you move around?

What kind of people were around you?

Did you have influence, or did you live simply?

What was the main theme of your life?

This is just a dream story, meant to be reflective. I know that it won't go as planned, but I also know that if we don't plan by looking at these questions in the first place, then it will go however it wants to. Our story should give us some insight into the things that we may want to change, right now.

I owned a successful website development business. My dream was to impact people's lives through books, training, and being awesome. So, I made the toughest decision of all: I gave up what I had, which was good, for something better. Not everyone needs to do this, but for me, I have discovered that it's difficult to do anything well when we are only half committed to it. I burned the ships intentionally and changed my career once again, but this time it's so I could move forward into my passion.

I knew this was the move to make after talking it out with someone I trusted. I've found that it's important to talk with multiple people because most will give you advice based on their own lenses. Change scares most people, so whenever discussing it, be sure to take what they are telling you with a grain of salt, even if they're someone trusted and respected. The decision needs to be your own. Ultimately, it's most important to talk with those people in your life whom will be most impacted by your changes.

I talked with my wife about making the change for a couple of years before taking the leap. We didn't discuss it all the time, but we would bring it up on various occasions. Dreaming together is a great way to strengthen a marriage, especially when there is space to pursue those dreams. On date nights, I would talk about things that I felt were wasting my talent, and the things I would enjoy doing. Ultimately, I can't know what I am going to like doing until trying something. There is power in taking the leap of faith. Sometimes it's forced like when I've lost a job, yet other times its just me going after a dream that I've cultivated with my wife. The power is in the doing.

HAVE FUN WITH YOUR HEALTH & FITNESS

I am a good healthy weight now, but it took me two times to get it right. My key was (you guessed it): having fun. When I lost 70 pounds I was roughly 280lbs as my heaviest at the time and I was tired of not feeling good. I had tried all kinds of diets and they all worked, but I would always gain it all back and then some. It was work and stressful and deprived me of one of my great joys: FOOD!

I love food! I love to cook and try all kinds of different things. I have always eaten healthy, plus a little junk food on the side, but I would just eat A LOT of food, and the portion-sizes were driving me out of control, regardless of if the food was healthy.

I was consuming more than my body could burn, so I packed on the pounds. The first time I lost a bunch of weight my goal was simply to reverse the process. I learned that the average American gained 1lb per month. I figured that if I took it easy with my portion-sizes and tried to lose 1lb per month, then I should be good to go. What ended up really happening was that I lost 15lbs the first week and then the rest of it over the next few months.

I made the decision that I was only going to do stuff that was fun. There were some simple things I could do right off. Number one was be content with one full plate of food instead of going back for seconds and thirds. The other thing was that I didn't like to work out at the gym, so I would find some soccer or basketball or some other kind of activity I could do instead of working out.

There is great power in positive peer pressure to hold us accountable for our journey's goals. Finding a group that we can have fun with while eating right and exercising makes all the difference in the world for permanent change. Going at something new alone isn't as fun as sharing the journey with other people.

I've seen early morning workout groups and mom walking groups and even pickup games at the park. There is always something we can do to have fun and get exercise in. Here's a tip if you've always wanted to learn how to do something: make getting in shape connected to it! Learn how to rock climb, surf, or sign up for some other activity that you've always wanted to learn how to do. Some may require being a certain weight like cycling or running a marathon, so in that case you're going to need to "train" with other fun activities to get your energy levels up. The key is to have fun.

Having fun with the food you eat is another good way to start eating healthy, especially if you're not used to it. It's so exciting to try new foods, but if your palette is used to fast food and prepackaged junk the good food won't taste right to you. Get your family involved. Try getting an Indian food cookbook and start at page one and make everything in it.

Being healthy should be fun, and even though there is work in the process, the overall outcome should be something you enjoy doing.

HAVE FUN WITH WORK

I've been an entrepreneur for most of the last 20 years. I've taken a few jobs in between, but for the most part I've gone at it on my own.

There isn't much in life more stressful than working. Either we're not making enough money, or we are doing well financially but it brings performance pressures along with it. It takes up the majority of our day and our mind. The average person returns from work completely emotionally spent. Which is boring and painful, and completely unnecessary.

It's no wonder that people are in poor health, physically, emotionally, and relationally. We spend so much of our time focused on something that makes us miserable. Since we have to earn a living and not working really isn't an option, then we better figure some way to fix this problem. The key component that seems to continually be missing is having fun.

The first thing is to love what you do. If you don't love it, then do something else. This isn't always prudent, and doesn't necessarily require that you quit your job. I worked as the promotions director for a cluster of radio stations, and when I first got the job the stations were in the middle of a major transformation. The General Manager at the time was hired to turn things around and create a platform for growth.

One of the moves he made baffled me. He took the person out of the finance department and moved her to the reception desk and he took the person from the reception desk and put her on the air. There were a handful of other moves that didn't require any hiring or firing, just some shuffling around. Even my position was newly available because of a shift in employee usage.

It worked! The station ratings tripled and all of the employees were a happy, cohesive team. I asked him about it and he said, "If someone isn't happy doing what they're doing that doesn't mean they need to go. In this case we just gave them what they wanted and they flourished because of it."

The key is to find something you love to do and do it. Let's say you're an entrepreneur and you build cabinets, for example. You may be tired of selling and quoting but you really enjoy working with the wood. So, hire someone to do the parts you don't like to do. If you're dealing with a part of your business that you can't stand, like the finances, then hire someone who can handle them.

Your business will grow and make space for the new expenditure. Sometimes it's as easy as hiring someone for a few hours a week as a consultant, temporarily for one project, or creating a new full-time position. Whatever it takes, you need to find a way to enjoy what you spend the majority of your time on.

If quitting your job is the only way, then you owe it to yourself and your employer to do it. You're not benefiting anyone working somewhere that you can't stand. Do whatever it takes: go back to school, or change careers altogether, or write that book that you've always dreamed of writing.

Making a drastic shift shouldn't be done because you can't stand your job; if that's the case, you'll end up setting a pattern of constantly finding something wrong. Go after your passion or you will end up in the same boat again. It never works to run from something that you don't like. Instead, you always need to have something good that you're running towards.

You only live once! You must do something that makes you come alive. You owe it to our self and to those around you. The world doesn't need you to fall in line, the world needs you to come alive. Once you have done this, then your impact will be immeasurable.

Go get it!

HAVE A FUN MARRIAGE

A great place to start this pursuit of coming alive is within our marital relationships. Marriage is fun! I love being married and my wife is truly amazing. Before I learned how to have fun in every area of my life, I liked being married, but it was work. I never wanted to do the dishes (I still don't like doing them) but I would happily clean the toilets. I dreaded anything resembling counseling and now I enjoy working on my marriage. I really couldn't say that being married was a blast before. Now, I can't help but smile every time I see my wife.

The key is having fun, yet again. It's not fun to fight, but it's important to communicate. Typically a blow-up fight comes from both people not being fully connected to themselves and their own needs. What happens is one person starts neglecting the other person, either on purpose or by accident, then the other person starts taking care of their own needs. Next thing you know, there is hurt and resentment and there is no end in sight. Communication starts to fade and depending on how committed the couple is to "making it work," the marriage can last for up to 25 years before coming to a fiery end with nothing but contempt left over.

My wife and I have made it one of our top priorities to have fun being together. We sit and talk for hours, or sometimes we sit and stare at the TV for hours. It's not important that we do or don't do certain things. What is important is that we are doing them together. If she feels ignored, then she says "I'm feeling ignored" and we talk about how to fix it or better yet I just listen to her.

It's amazing what can happen in a marriage when we're able to just listen to the other person without judging their motives. It's easy to try to analyze what is the person "really" saying, but it's not going to help. If they aren't actually saying it then they don't feel comfortable opening up. Do you know what the best way to get someone to open up is? Go have fun together.

It's easy to do something I like doing or she likes doing. Finding something we both like doing was more challenging when learning how to enjoy being married. Now it doesn't really matter what the activity is, just being together is fun. Our son has soccer tournaments 4 hours away every month, so guess what we do with that? We make it into a mini vacation and spend time talking and dreaming together.

Whatever problem you think you might have, there's always enough time to start having fun, whether it's marriage, parenting, or other roles in life.

HAVE FUN PARENTING

My son told me that he likes his new teacher because she makes learning fun. I couldn't help but smile and I asked him to elaborate. Why is it better to have fun when learning? There were a few of his friends around and they all told me the same thing: "When we're bored, it's hard to concentrate. We don't learn as much and some of us end up misbehaving."

BINGO! The key to parenting is to not get bored with the necessary routines and instead have fun doing it. My kids are so much better off now that I have found the joy of being a dad. They listen and do what they are asked to do. They go to bed on time and when they have to do something they really don't want to do, they will give me a fit, but in the end they will do it anyway.

My wife likes me more now too as a husband because of the dad that I am becoming. Everyone likes to be around someone having fun. It's tough to stomach a grouch, and it causes more problems than is necessary in a family dynamic.

I used to be that grouch, and would let it reflect into my parenting. My problem was, I couldn't take "it" anymore, and was short-fused about anything that occurred around me. Every noise, every misstep felt like a direct attack on my soul. My reactions then affected the kids and created a domino effect of misbehavior. Once I learned how to enjoy the mistakes and see the stuff my kids did as normal kid stuff, I began my path to freedom.

I still get irritated, annoyed and pushed but the outcome is not an explosion of emotion like it used to be. I don't suppress, but I also don't let the little things attack my very being like they used to. Let's face it, kids are great at pressing our buttons. They know what they're doing, and at the same time they have no clue what they're doing. As a parent, it's my job to help them learn from their mistakes. However, no learning happens when there is fear.

My oldest son is so good for me, reminding me to keep myself in check. He said, "Dad I can't concentrate when you get upset." So if I want him to concentrate, then I have to leave Hulk in the closet. Making games and contests help the kids perform their tasks quickly and they respond really well to them. If I'm in a hurry to get one of them to practice, they are more likely to rush into the car if I say something like the first one in the car get's to choose the radio station. It may cause a bit of dissension because someone will be last, but it does the job and creates a fun exciting way to get to our destination.

Find joy in being a parent. Remind yourself how exciting your dreams were for what you would get to do with the kids before you had them. Think about when they were little babies and all kinds of possibilities were before them. Think about what your dream family looked like when you began planning for a family and then go make that happen. I learned that the only thing keeping me from having fun as a dad was me deciding not to have fun.

If we have fun as a parent, your children will be happier, listen more, do better in school and treat each other and themselves with more respect. Make hearing about their day a fun thing to do, and ask them questions that stir up dreams inside them. If we teach our children to enjoy their life, they will stay away from all those things that we as parents want them to stay away from.

What areas of your life do you need to have more fun in?

How can you incorporate fun tasks while doing the un-fun ones?

Can you think of things that you enjoy doing that you aren't doing?

THE TOP REGRETS PEOPLE HAVE AT THE END OF THEIR LIVES

If you have never seen the movie Braveheart by Mel Gibson, do it. The main character William Wallace, has to face the English army in an attempt to free Scotland from the tyranny of the King of England. The odds are against them, they are outnumbered, under armed, and out classed. The clans of Scotland showed up to the battlefield but started to leave once they realized it was a death sentence. Wallace replied against a shout from the crowd that asked, "Fight? Against that? No! We will run. And we will live."

> Aye, fight and you may die. Run, and you'll live... at least a while. And dying in your beds, many years from now, would you be willin' to trade ALL the days, from this day to that, for one chance, just one chance, to come back here and tell our enemies that they may take our lives, but they'll never take... OUR FREEDOM!
>
> -William Wallace, Braveheart (1995)

Wallace's reply that we only have one chance to die for our freedoms makes a simple point. Yes, if you leave you will live for now. Maybe you make it all the way to the end of your life. But when you lay there dying is it worth it to have lived your whole life afraid of finding your freedom? Will you regret not fighting when you still had the chance? Is it worth the risk of dying now so you get the future you've always dreamed of? The answer was, they charged and won the battle.

We all have an English army that we're figuratively fighting in our own lives. There are daily battles that we face before we die, and yet when doing a simple internet search interviewing those towards the end of their life, there are five main statements that were mentioned as regrets by people when asked what they wished they would have done differently.

I should have let myself be happier.

As we learned earlier, long term happiness is 90% determined by how you view and interact with the world. The Ancient Greeks described happiness (eudaimonia) as the freedom that comes from being wealthy or receiving some sort of good fortune in either health or finances. We learned from Amit Kumar that using money to buy experiences improves our overall enjoyment of life. Spending money on stuff does not make us happy, but it's all about creating stories and experiences that we can share with others that ups our joy.

The key then to allowing happiness in your life is to go for it! Get yourself an optimistic outlook and start experiencing the world around you. If you're all set up with every hour of your day booked from now until Christmas, then you better make some changes. You need to have space for spontaneity, time to sit and enjoy the life that you're creating for yourself.

Happiness is not an emotion; it is a state of being. There is the happy emotion, but like all emotions it's fleeting. To truly be happy you need to be in a state of happiness, and you need to set yourself up to enjoy life. Make having fun a priority.

At the end of your life you should be able to look back and say, "I've had my ups and downs, but my personal legend is everything I had hoped it would be." I know for me, I'm willing to do what it takes to make that a reality.

I wish I didn't work so hard

I'm ok with working hard for a time but this regret is about working hard all of the time. I've found that people who work hard all of the time find it difficult to rest. Most of the Type A personalities that I know can't sit on a beach and enjoy it without being productive. Regardless of personality types, anyone can find ways to have fun and enjoy their life if they are willing to teach themselves how to relax. For some, that comes naturally, while for others it might take more energy to discover the power of having fun and how it increases your chances of success.

I used to not be good at finishing projects, so I would say self-deprecating things like, "I'm a starter not a finisher" to justify my actions. That was my past, but it was never true. I have learned how to finish, and finish strong. The truth is that I'm a pioneer. I love breaking new ground and yet I still find the fine details to be monotonous and boring. But, because they are required to complete a task, I learned how to finish. Now it's no longer a problem for me.

The Type A "never stop" personality can learn how to rest and enjoy a time of doing nothing. Remember the seasons? It's important to learn how to take time to enjoy the fruits of our labor. If we don't, we will live in a constant state of stress and be physically incapable of enjoying our lives.

I would have expressed my feelings more.

This takes courage, and often that is used when talking about this point. How many times do we lack the courage to express what's truly in our heart? Our fear creeps in and in the order of keeping the peace or not rocking the boat we would rather keep silent then be honest.

I think the big one here is learning that our feelings are

valid. Like I wrote about earlier, they aren't always accurate, but they are ours, they have a reason and are valid. YOU are valid and your feelings are a part of you.

If I get angry, it's ok to express my anger. What's not ok, however, is to punish the people around me either physically or emotionally. Learning how to properly express feelings can be the key to learning how to have the courage to be more open.

How many times do we want to say something that has been bothering us for years but because it's been years, it's almost impossible to do it? I want to encourage you to let go. Sometimes just acknowledging our own feelings inside is enough but most of the time we need expression.

We can come up with tools for how to express our feelings and always stay clear. When I'm feeling stressed or anxious, I get outside. It could be going for a hike or simply a walk around the block. If I'm feeling stifled, I'll play music or do something creative. We all have to sort out for ourselves what it takes to get us back to a place of clarity. Most of the time, a conversation is in order and setting up the rules so we can feel safe to do that is important. Either way if you can process the feelings alone first by using one of these kinds of tools then when you do express your feelings you will do so from a better place.

I wish I had stayed in touch with my friends.

Relationship is the cornerstone of a happy life. I'm good at relationships, and one of the reasons why this is that I have seen is because I always try to put people first. So many times people burn relationships because they have a fight, or reach an impasse and it's easier to just "never mind" the friendship or let it fizzle out. The problem is, people are different and come from different places and operate from different values. Every soul is unique.

It's not so much about relationships taking work but taking LOVE. We need to consider the other person's feelings and make sure that we are being as respectful of our self as we are of them. It takes listening and being a part of their lives. Most importantly, it takes forgiveness because most relationships will have hiccups along the way. Learning how to discuss what needs to happen and then moving on is very important.

As we learned previously, the relating of stories is key to long term happiness. Having someone to talk about old stories with is very healing for the soul, and does wonders for the psyche. Staying in touch with old friends is a way to stay connected to your past story. It's also one of the best paths to joy.

I wish I had lived a life other than what was expected of me and be true to myself.

If you haven't seen this theme while reading, then you should go back and read it again. It's so important for your overall enjoyment of life that you spend time connecting with yourself. The true you, not the one that is full of pain and struggle.

I've talked with many people about discovering themselves, and I'm going to tell you right now that there is no onion to peel. If you start peeling back the layers of an onion you still get an onion. The true You is the one that God says you are, not something made up through a lens of pain and a history of abuse.

You teach others how to treat you and how to interact with you. If you have a bad family dynamic, it's because you are allowing it to continue. You don't need to go hash it out, although I'm always in favor of communication, you get to set the rules for what you will put up with and what you won't. If they are having a conversation that you don't approve of, just remove yourself from that conversation.

Regardless of what expectations people put on us, only you can live your life. Only you know what you want it to look like and what impact you want to have on those around you. You are the master of your fate, and the designer of your destiny. Create the life that you want. It's your story and your turn, so what kind of life do you want to have when you get to the end?

> "I am the master of my fate; I am the captain of my soul."
>
> - William Ernest Henley

URIM AND THUMMIM

In *The Alchemist*, I was introduced to the concept of Urim and Thummim. These are actual stones, one black and one white, that were in the Breastplate of Aaron in the Bible which represents a really interesting concept of decision making. In the book, Santiago (the main character) was supposed to use these stones whenever he was faced with a difficult decision. He would take them out of their pouch, hold them in his hand and ultimately make a decision which then helps him move forward. The biblical version is the same, they were to represent the decision making process for the priesthood.

Whenever there is a decision to make, we can either choose one way or the other. One way isn't necessarily wrong and the other way right; they are simply two different paths to choose. Regardless of which direction we choose, we are creating a new path that never existed before. Choosing nothing is still making a choice, and choosing the one way doesn't necessarily take away the other, just the pathway to get there.

Urim and Thummim are translated as Light and Truth and they are featured on the coat of arms for the University of Yale with the inscription Lux et Veritas, "Light & Truth." We are the ones that have to make the decision. The idea is similar to the story of King Solomon and the baby.

Two women had babies about the same time. Shortly after birth, one woman rolled over onto her baby in her sleep and killed the infant. Realizing what she had done, she quickly swapped her baby out with the other mother's child. In the morning, when the other woman realized the dead baby next to her wasn't hers she began to argue with the one who lost her child. They went before the king to relay the story and get rights to the child. Solomon thought for a while and said, "Bring me a sword. Since we can't agree who is right, I will cut the baby in two and both of you can have half." The mother of the already dead child agreed, but quickly the biological mother refused and said, "Let her keep the baby; just don't kill it!"

Solomon knew then who the real mother was, took the baby and gave it to the mother who was willing to give it up.

Clearly Solomon had no intention of cutting a baby in half, but he knew the heart of a mother. The woman would rather not get to raise the child as long as she knew it would be safe.

To me, this shows the concept of Urim and Thummim. Simply making a decision wouldn't be good enough; he had to let the right decision present itself by pursuing truth through light.

While you may be going through a transitional time in your life while learning how to prioritize fun and begin to live the life that you've always wanted, remember that the truth you know now may not be through the lens of light. The more you heal your soul, the better your decision making process will become. Start simply.

HAVE FUN!

Chapter 09
FUN EXTRAS

In this fun extras chapter you will find some articles, free downloads, and added information that was requested by readers. This first article "How To Be Happy" was written in response to some people I was coaching that specifically asked if I could teach them "how to be happy." If you would like some more articles check my blog at Ryan8.com.

How To Be Happy

Happiness is a state of being and a state of mind in harmony. You can have everything in the world that "makes you happy" and still be miserable. You can seem happy on the outside like Robin Williams (RIP) and still be tormented on the inside. You can fill your life and your world with all the right stuff and not be happy. You can do and say all the right things that should make you happy and still be miserable

**Here are some happy emotions:
Joy, Peace, Love, Satisfaction, Relaxation, etc....**

We can feel the emotion of being happy, which we call joy, but to live and operate from happiness we need to have our emotions and our physical responses in harmony.

IF we get joy from coffee and yet we never drink it because it's bad for us, we start denying our self that joy, so that then every time we smell it at meetings, restaurants, or our spouse makes in the morning we will feel a loss. That denial of something we love will cause us to fall out of a state of happiness. We will actually begin to grieve the loss of that part of our life that brings us joy. How many times have we stopped doing something that we enjoy because we were told it is bad for us only to go back to it again? I can tell you this...

IF we stop doing something that brings us happy emotions, we will begin to grieve the loss and start to slip into a place of depression. A great example of this is Postpartum Depression. I believe that women who experience this are grieved from the Loss of being pregnant. Not that the Joy of the baby is less or worse or any of that, but there is a special bond that I've noticed with pregnant women that NO ONE else can experience, which is special and magical.

What's my point? The only way to stop doing something that "brings me joy," like eating ice cream at 11pm, is to get a proper mindset and understanding about why we do it and what we are GAINING from it. Only once we understand what we are getting from it, then will we understand WHY we do it.

IF our why is more powerful than the joy emotion, in which we will gain from NOT doing it, then stopping will be a challenge and can cause depression.

The opposite can be true as well.

IF we are excited about something enough, we can easily let go of what we had to get to that "something." For example, if someone really wants that car being advertised online, he or she would be willing to let go of MONEY and TIME to earn enough to get the car. Will we grieve the loss of our time and money? Possibly; it's called buyer's remorse.

IF we fill our life with exciting anticipations, we can mimic the happiness state of being, but it's not sustainable. We will be on vacation, enjoying our hard earned epic adventure and laying on the beach thinking…."I'm bored." WHY? It's because happiness is a state of BEING, not an emotion. It's important that we get our mind right about what is important. Happiness is finding joy in the planning, the process, and the outcome of whatever it is that we are doing.

WHAT DOES THIS ALL MEAN?

Well, for me it's a mantra... BE HAPPY! Life is worth living and it's exciting and there are amazing things to do and see and people to connect with. So be happy. Nature is amazing if you spend any time in it and the world that God created, it is spectacular. Be happy that you get to experience it. People are truly remarkable and the MAJORITY of them want to be good and nice and helpful members of society. That right there is all the knowledge that we need to be happy.

Our BS (Belief System) is what keeps us from living life from a STATE OF HAPPINESS. So next time we find ourselves experiencing BS, we need to shift our focus onto something that will help us become happy instead!

THE HOW TO

#1 - FEEL

Your KEY to getting to the place of happiness is to FEEL emotions. It's ok! When it's time to grieve...grieve. When it's time to laugh... laugh. When you are feeling anxious, go ahead and give yourself permission to FEEL it. I mean really feel it.

EVERY DECISION YOU MAKE IS EMOTIONAL, THERE IS NO SUCH THING AS A RATIONAL DECISION!

Why am I so passionate about that? Because it's true! Even if we are making a "rational decision" it's still based on our emotions. It's never purely numerical. Don't believe me? Let's look at sports. College football got rid of the BCS system which is ALL based on numbers and computer analysis to decide rankings and quality of teams. It was eliminated because there are intangibles that a computer couldn't quantify. For example: heart or swagger, or pick your sporting terminology.

Another example is the law requires a Judge to interpret it and whether or not it applies to the situation. Including passing sentence which can be an arbitrary number allowing for human adjustment. NONE of that is rational. We can rationalize our decisions based on a set of common understandings like science but ultimately we make decisions from our emotions.

SO WHY THE TANGENT – I want to make something very clear to you. If you are stuck somewhere it is because you are either AFRAID to do something else or you have SHAME about doing it.

FEAR is NOT just an acronym for False Expectations Appearing Real, FEAR is real. When you feel fear your best course of action is to recognize that your body is creating a physical reaction to that emotion and you will make dumb decisions until you can come to terms with the emotion.

THE EXAMPLE – My oldest son and daughter had a fear of the dark that started around 3 years old. On separate occasions I was able to help them overcome that fear. With this story:

The dark is scary huh? (nods) Did you know that Daddy is afraid of the dark also? (shakes head, no) That's right, I am afraid of the dark but you don't see me acting that way do you? (shakes head, no) I'll tell you a secret that I learned.

I know that there is nothing in the dark different from when the light is on. I know that because we can check. See the light is on, and there is nothing there. The light is off, and we are afraid of it again. Why? I don't know. But, what I was able to do was to understand that I am having some fear about it and make the decision that FEAR

WILL NOT BEAT ME!

You are so strong son, and brave. And I KNOW that you have enough courage to say to the dark that it will not beat you either. You are powerful enough and brave enough that even though you are afraid, you will NOT let that fear beat you. We know there is nothing there but it still is scary, so the only way to not be trapped in our bed when we're scared is to be braver (I know, not a word but the kids like it) than the fear. Do you think you can do that? (nods)

It only took one of these conversations to get rid of the night light forever. It has worked on both my son and my daughter now. Does that mean they aren't scared? NOPE. They still have a fear of the dark, just like I do (yes to this day I am still afraid of the dark, and NO nothing ever happened to me in the dark). But, we are courageous and carry on into the night anyway.

SO, feel your emotions! When you are happy, really feel it. When you are excited, really feel it. When you are sad, angry, etc… really feel them. This is a huge part of enjoying life, knowing that all of the parts of life add to our own story.

Allow yourself to have your moment and take the time to process the who, why, where, what, how's of it all. You will be amazed at the results of this.

2. CHOOSE

Happiness is a choice. We can choose happiness over any other state of being. When you are down and beat up and not in a good place, that can be a difficult choice but it's still a choice.

DO something about the emotion you just felt. Typically REACTING to a situation is a bad thing, but as you begin to take action and respond to the emotions with intention your whole world will start to open up. Even babies smile…why? Did they see us smile enough to start learning that behavior. In my experience…nope. They were born with the ability to smile in response to joyful emotions.

Heck, even animals smile… So that type of reacting is great! It's a natural response. So ALL the natural reaction responses are more healthy than the planned action responses. HOWEVER, you can train yourself to react differently than our natural responses as humans. OK, that's enough of that, on to action.

If we take the scary darkness story from above, where is the action in that story? It's in deciding to be courageous. The action of courage is what overcomes the emotion of fear. In fact every time my kids go to bed and conquer their fear with courage it actually makes them more courageous in other areas of their life.

What Does That Have To Do With Being Happy?

Typically we will react to a situation based upon the paradigm that we have created for ourselves. People who were abused tend to get into a defensive position when there is yelling or tense situations. These folks have a reason to act that way, and are right to do so because of the life that they have been dealt to that point. The issue is that once you are past that part of your life it can still control your happiness factor. Our lives and life experiences really do create the people we are today. So the only way to get past negative habits is to create a new paradigm.

Today I choose to be HAPPY. I realize that Happiness is a choice and even if I don't always feel HAPPY, I will always choose HAPPY. I give myself permission to have bad days and I give myself permission to have good days. I choose to be HAPPY.

NOW WE PUT IT ALL TOGETHER

So what's the secret? There really isn't a secret or key that will be universal for all of us, but I have found some commonalities that we can learn from.

Life is meant to be enjoyed. All of life. From the amazing highs of your child being born, to the lows of losing a loved one, it's all part of the same life. We are here on this earth for a certain period of time and regardless of your belief system I can guarantee 1 thing… Today Will End… and what you did today will be in the past.

You get 1 shot at life. Your kids are only little once. You only get to be 25 once. You only have that great moment of your life once. You may have more kids, and more moments…. or no kids and sad moments, but it will ALL only happen once.

SO…

What are you doing today that will echo into your tomorrow? When the final curtain closes will you look back on your life in wonder and amazement of the greatness of it, or will you look back and think, "I made it."

The reason I bring this up as part of the how to be Happy is because life is a gift that we GET to live. We don't HAVE to do or be anything. There is no greater purpose for our lives than to be ourselves and enjoy every second of it. The purposes and destinies that we gain along the way are part of us creating our own personal legend. We have a choice about what life we want to live and which way to go almost every day.

I chose to be happy…I choose to live fulfilled….I chose to enjoy my life.

I will not allow my past, present or future be dictated to me. I will live a life worth living, and I will choose the path that works for me.

Now is your time, and now is your turn!

Serendipity

Serendipity is a fortunate happenstance or pleasant surprise. It is luck that takes the form of finding valuable or pleasant things that are not looked for. Just writing that sentence makes me excited about what's going to happen next, and it's not because I know what to expect. It's the excitement of the unknown that I find thrilling!.

Despite what some may think, serendipity is not actually something "accidentally" happening to you. It is being actively open to finding what you never anticipated finding. If you're not open, then you're likely not to recognize the fortunate happenstance. The "accident" will come and go and you will have never known without first seeking for a lesson or correlation to what happens in your life's events.

One of the ways that I am actively open to finding something that I wasn't looking for is to be available to have my day interrupted. I know it's not terribly efficient to stop what you're doing so you can have a conversation with that guy at Starbucks that won't stop talking, but on more than one occasion it has led to some good things.

For example, I had been thinking about getting some saddle bags for my Harley Davidson motorcycle, and this guy started yakin' in my ear about his Harley. Because I allowed the interruption, he ended up giving me a set of brand new Harley Davidson brand saddle bags. I'm not saying that serendipity leads to free swag, but sometimes the most unlikely of solutions comes from taking the time to be present with those around you.

Another way that I'm actively open to have something fall in my lap is to be generous with my time, stuff and money. We have been given some amazing things for simply being the kind of people who "deserve" it. I don't much like that term because most people deserve grace, but it's easier to think of someone who is generous when it comes time to giving a blessing.

I like to have fun at the grocery store and look for things that I can bring back to surprise my wife and kids. I use the principle of serendipity to lead me to the right gift. It could be a sale rack, or a display with something on it. Or I might go down a specific aisle knowing that there is likely something there that will catch my eye. The key is to be open to the discovery.

As a matter of fact, I'm known for being a good gift giver. One of the reasons is that I allow the right gift to present itself. Pun intended. :) When it comes time for someone's birthday or Christmas, I put myself in the right place to find the right present. I consider the personality of the person I am shopping for then I simply follow my nose.

I use serendipity in business all the time. I can't tell you how many times I'll be at a coffee shop or at the beach or some place where I'm not trying to do business and I'll have a conversation that leads to business. And sometimes, the greatest blessings come from our greatest struggles. I remember a story that my broker told me, when I used to sell commercial real estate, about the 1 time in 25 years that he was sued. He told me that on his way to the courthouse he ran into someone in the hall and they got to talking about business. That conversation led to his biggest sale of the year.

These stories coupled with my own experiences are what led me to adopt serendipity as a key component of having fun in all areas of my life. Coaching my kids' soccer teams has brought me business, playing beach volleyball, body surfing with friends, and even solo hiking in the wilderness has all brought me business in one form or another.

I remember one time I was on a solo backpacking trip in the Sierra Nevada mountains and I ran into someone I knew from over 6 hrs away. Now the likelihood of running into anyone out there was slim but to find someone that I knew was really not on my radar. You could call it luck or a mere coincidence, but honestly these types of things happen way too often to chalk it up to randomness.

Allowing serendipity to have it's place in your life is a key to having fun. I'll be fully in the moment with my kids soccer and then someone will come up to me afterwards and we'll start talking. Next thing you know, I'll have a new connection for a business deal that I didn't anticipate.

Relationships are a great area to be ready for serendipity. If my wife says something like, "Ugh, I need to do the dishes before I can relax!" What a great opportunity for me to show my love for her and go help. If my kids say something like, "I'm bored" aren't they really saying "Play with me!"?

It's important that we are consciously looking for opportunities to connect in relationships. It is in those moments where you will find out how deep your love for each other is. It's those moments where you will discover all the really cool qualities that your kids have. It's in those moments where you will find life.

BE READY FOR YOUR MOMENT!

FREEBIES

**FUNdamental Worksheets &
Special Product Discounts**
www.ryan8.com/fundamental

Ryan's 50/50 Workout Plan
www.ryan8.com/theFUNdiet

I would love to hear from all of you.

Visit the website www.ryan8.com and send me a message.

NOTES

Introduction. *Kung Fu Panda*. Dir. Mark Osborne, John Stevenson. Perf. Jack Black, Ian McShane, Angelina Jolie. DreamWorks Animation, 2008.

Chapter 1. fundamental. (n.d.). *Collins English Dictionary - Complete & Unabridged 10th Edition*. Retrieved October 24, 2016 from Dictionary.com website http://www.dictionary.com/browse/fundamental

Chapter 1. Liu D, Diorio J, Tannenbaum B, Caldji C, Francis D, Freedman A, Sharma S, Pearson D, Plotsky PM, Meaney MJ (1997) Maternal care, hippocampal glucocorticoid receptors, and hypothalamic-pituitary-adrenal responses to stress. Science 277: 1659–1662.

Chapter 1. John Salamone - "Dopamine: it's not about pleasure anymore"

Chapter 1."Dopamine: Biological activity". IUPHAR/BPS guide to pharmacology. International Union of Basic and Clinical Pharmacology. Retrieved 29 January 2016.

Chapter 1. Weisman O, Zagoory-Sharon O, Feldman R (September 2012). "Intranasal oxytocin administration is reflected in human saliva". Psychoneuroendocrinology. 37 (9): 1582–6. doi:10.1016/j.psyneuen.2012.02.014. PMID 22436536.

Chapter 1. Coila, Bridgett. "Effects of Serotonin on the Body." LiveStrong. n.p., 20 June. 2010. Web. 11 Aug. 2013.

Chapter 1. Goldstein A, Lowery PJ (September 1975). "Effect of the opiate antagonist naloxone on body temperature in rats". Life Sciences. 17 (6): 927–31. doi:10.1016/0024-3205(75)90445-2. PMID 1195988.

Chapter 1. "Vitamin B-3: Niacin and Its Amide" by A. Hoffer, M.D., Ph.D.

Chapter 2. fun. (n.d.). *Collins English Dictionary* - Complete & Unabridged 10th Edition. Retrieved October 24, 2016 from Dictionary.com website http://www.dictionary.com/browse/fun

Chapter 2. TedTalk - Tyler Dewitt "Hey Science Teachers - Make it fun". Nov. 2012

Chapter 2. Hoffman, Miles (1997). "*Syncopation*". National Symphony Orchestra. NPR. Retrieved 13 July 2009.

Chapter 2. Imposter Syndrome - Clance, P.R.; Imes, S.A. (1978). "The imposter phenomenon in high achieving women: dynamics and therapeutic intervention.". Psychotherapy: Theory, Research and Practice.

Chapter 3. challenging. (n.d.). *Collins English Dictionary*. Complete & Unabridged 10th Edition. Retrieved October 24, 2016 from Dictionary.com http://www.dictionary.com/browse/challenging

Chapter 3. Edgar A. Guest - *Don't Quit*. 3rd of March 1921

Chapter 3. Winston Churchill - *Never Give In* October 29, 1941.

Chapter 4. prioritize. (n.d.). *Dictionary.com Unabridged*. Retrieved October 24, 2016 from Dictionary.com website http://www.dictionary.com/browse/prioritize

Chapter 4. *Luke* 16:1-9 New American Standard Bible (NASB) Copyright © 1960, 1962, 1963, 1968, 1971, 1972, 1973, 1975, 1977, 1995 by The Lockman Foundation

Chapter 4. Meghan M. Biro, "Happy Employees = Hefty Profits" on Forbes.com

Chapter 4. Happy Chewbacca - https://youtu.be/0jjlXzWho9w

Chapter 4. Edgar A. Guest - *Don't Quit*. 3rd of March 1921

Chapter 4. Maslow, A.H. (1943). "A theory of human motivation". Psychological Review. 50 (4): 370–96. doi:10.1037/h0054346 – via psychclassics.yorku.ca.

Chapter 4. Amit Kumar, Ph.D. Cornell University - Quotes taken from the website *www.kumar-amit.com*

Chapter 5. empower. (n.d.). *Online Etymology Dictionary*. Retrieved October 24, 2016 from Dictionary.com website http://www.dictionary.com/browse/empower

Chapter 5. Lieb, E.H., Yngvason, J. (1999). The physics and mathematics of the second law of thermodynamics, Physics Reports, 314: 1–96, p. 55–56.

Chapter 5. *Ecclesiastes* 9:7 - New American Standard Bible (NASB) Copyright © 1960, 1962, 1963, 1968, 1971, 1972, 1973, 1975, 1977, 1995 by The Lockman Foundation

Chapter 5. *Hook*. Dir. Steven Spielberg. Perf. Dustin Hoffman, Robin Williams, Julia Roberts. Amblin Entertainment, 1991.

Chapter 5. Edgar A. Guest - *Don't Quit*. 3rd of March 1921

Chapter 6. transform. (n.d.). *Dictionary.com Unabridged*. Retrieved October 24, 2016 from Dictionary.com website http://www.dictionary.com/browse/transform

Chapter 6. Harvard University's Positive Psychology 1504 by Tal Ben-Shahar (PhD)

Chapter 6. Shawn Achor - *The Happiness Advantage*. 2010

Chapter 7. heal. (n.d.). *Online Etymology Dictionary*. Retrieved October 24, 2016 from Dictionary.com website http://www.dictionary.com/browse/heal

Chapter 7. Vallfors B. *Acute, Subacute and Chronic Low Back Pain: Clinical Symptoms, Absenteeism and Working Environment*. Scan J Rehab Med Suppl 1985; 11: 1-98.

Chapter 7. "Food Detectives" Hosted by Ted Allen - *The effects of MSG - (Episode: OF0204)*

Chapter 7. *Healing Back Pain* by Dr. Sarno

Chapter 7. Philippians 4:8 - New American Standard Bible (NASB)Copyright © 1960, 1962, 1963, 1968, 1971, 1972, 1973, 1975, 1977, 1995 by The Lockman Foundation

Chapter 7. Harvard University's Positive Psychology 1504 by Tal Ben-Shahar (PhD)

Chapter 7. Nissa Andrews - *Pain Free Child Birth*. 2006.

Chapter 8. story. (n.d.). *Online Etymology Dictionary*. Retrieved October 24, 2016 from Dictionary.com website http://www.dictionary.com/browse/story

Chapter 8. Paulo Coelho - *The Alchemist*. 2007 - I enjoyed his book very much.

Chapter 8. *A Prospective Study of Holiday Weight Gain*

Jack A. Yanovski, M.D., Ph.D., Susan Z. Yanovski, M.D., Kara N. Sovik, B.S., Tuc T. Nguyen, M.S., Patrick M. O'Neil, Ph.D., and Nancy G. Sebring, M.Ed., R.D.

N Engl J Med 2000; 342:861-867March 23, 2000DOI: 10.1056/NEJM200003233421206

Chapter 8. *Braveheart*. Dir. Mel Gibson movies. Perf. Mel Gibson, Sophie Marceau, Patrick McGoohan. Icon Entertainment International, 1995. - One of my all time favorite

ABOUT THE AUTHOR

RYAN ANDREWS is a business owner, speaker, consultant and entrepreneur. He was the co-host of a #1 comedy podcast and a #1 psychology podcast. He is a worship pastor for over 17 years and has been all over the world helping people find their passion. His pursuit is to represent a life on fire.

Ryan is one of those people that you meet and immediately want to engage. He has learned through a lifetime of overcoming challenges how to enjoy life to the fullest and he discovered that his passion is helping others to find what makes them come alive. He has completed the Ironman 70.3 triathlon in Lake Tahoe, and is an endurance athlete competing in olympic distance and cross country triathlons. He is currently training to climb Mt. Kilimanjaro.

Ryan grew up in Hawaii, and lives in Redding, CA with his beautiful wife Nissa, and their 4 children.

www.ryan8.com

FREEBIES

**FUNdamental Worksheets &
Special Product Discounts**
www.ryan8.com/fundamental

Ryan's 50/50 Workout Plan
www.ryan8.com/theFUNdiet

I would love to hear from all of you.

Visit the website www.ryan8.com and send me a message.

www.ingramcontent.com/pod-product-compliance
Lightning Source LLC
LaVergne TN
LVHW051601070426
835507LV00021B/2705